W9-BLJ-795

CliffsNotes™

Investing for the First Time

By Tracey Longo

IN THIS BOOK

- Invest successfully the first time
- Learn how to meet your investing goals
- Find investments that are right for you
- Track the progress of your investments
- Reinforce what you learn in CliffsNotes Resource Center and online at www.cliffsnotes.com

IDG Books Worldwide, Inc.
An International Data Group Company
Foster City, CA • Chicago, IL • Indianapolis, IN • New York, NY

IDG
BOOKS
WORLDWIDE

About the Author

Tracey Longo has 15 years of journalism experience, specializing in personal finance and money management topics. She covers personal finance issues for national publications including The Washington Post and Investor's Business Daily, and her work has been regularly syndicated by The New York Times.

Publisher's Acknowledgments

Editorial

Senior Project Editor: Mary Goodwin

Acquisitions Editors: Mark Butler, Karen Hansen

Copy Editors: Patricia Yuu Pan, Linda S. Stark

Technical Editor: Ellen Rogin, CPA, CFP

Production

Proofreader: York Production Services

Indexer: York Production Services

IDG Books Indianapolis Production Department

Table of Contents

INTRODUCTION

Welcome to the world of investing! It's an exciting world where you can make your money work for you. You can take your hard-earned cash and make it grow, helping you to achieve your financial goals, such as sending your children to college, living comfortably, and creating a secure retirement.

You can make all sorts of investments (for example, options trading, gas and oil ventures, collectibles, precious metals, futures, and real estate), but in this book I focus on some of the most common and accessible financial instruments.

With a little planning, almost everyone can get into investing. All you need is a set of firm goals and a little help to show you how you can best reach those goals. That's where this book comes in.

Why Do You Need this Book?

Can you answer yes to any of these questions?

- Do you need to learn about investing options fast?
- Don't have time to read 500 pages on investing?
- Are you unsure where to turn for simple, effective information on investing?
- Are you perplexed about exactly how to build an investment plan?

If so, then CliffsNotes *Investing for the First Time* is for you!

How to Use this Book

The beauty of this book is that it takes the guesswork out of your decision making. It gives you the tools you need to identify your true financial goals, regardless of how lofty they may seem. Then you get crucial information on how you can meet those goals using the variety of investments that are available, including savings accounts, Individual Retirement Accounts (IRAs), stocks, bonds, mutual funds, and real estate, among others.

This book is designed to help you understand your investing choices on a fundamental level in light of your own goals, needs, and comfort level. Instead of wondering how different investment products work, CliffsNotes *Investing for the First Time* gives you the fundamentals on the products that are available to you, what they can and can't do, what type of performance and risk you can expect, and how you can analyze investments to ensure that you select those that best meet your needs.

In addition, the book tells you where to turn for on-target, up-to-the-minute analysis and even provides you with a primer on how to get into each different type of investment.

You're the boss here. You get to decide how to use this book. You can either read the book from cover to cover or just look for the information you want and put it back on the shelf for later. However, I'll tell you about a few ways I recommend to search for your topic(s):

- Use the index in the back of the book to find what you're looking for.

- Flip through the book looking for your topic in the running heads at the top of the page.

- Look for your topic in the table of contents in the front of the book.

- Look at the In This Chapter list at the beginning of each chapter.

- Look for additional information in the CliffsNotes Resource Center.

- Or flip through the book until you find what you're looking for — because we organized the book in a logical, task-oriented way.

Also, to find important information quickly, you can look for icons strategically placed in the text. Here's a description of the icons you can find in this book:

- When you see a Remember icon, make a mental note of this text — it's is worth keeping in mind.

- A Tip icon flags a helpful hint, a secret, or valuable advice.

- The Warning icon alerts you to something that could be dangerous, requires special caution, or should be avoided.

Don't Miss Our Web Site

Keep up with the exciting world of investing by visiting the CliffsNotes Web site at www.cliffsnotes.com. Here's what you can find:

- Interactive tools that are fun and informative
- Links to interesting Web sites
- Additional resources to help you continue your learning

At www.cliffsnotes.com, you can even register for a new feature called *CliffsNotes Daily*, which offers you newsletters on a variety of topics, delivered right to your e-mail inbox each business day.

If you haven't yet discovered the Internet and are wondering how to get online, pick up *Getting On the Internet,* new from CliffsNotes. You can learn just what you need to make your online connection quickly and easily. See you at www.cliffsnotes.com!

CHAPTER 1
SETTING REALISTIC GOALS AND EXPECTATIONS

IN THIS CHAPTER

- Understanding risk and reward
- Writing down your goals
- Understanding the importance of compound interest
- Determining how much you need to invest to reach your goals

In this chapter, you can learn about the starting points of thoughtful investing. You can also learn why you need to determine your goals and get started on your investment plan as early as possible.

Understanding Risk and Reward

What has drawn you to investing? Maybe it's the raging stock market of the 1990s. Or maybe you're enticed by the idea that you can put your money to work for you by investing it.

Although the benefits of investing are often made clear in success story after success story in advertisements, magazines, newspapers, and online Web sites devoted to investing, it's important to remember that there is no gain without potential pain. That means that when you invest your money, you can lose part or all of it.

Actually, rewards and risks are usually closely related. The greater an investment's potential for reward, the greater the potential for risk and actual loss. The high-flying stock that earned a 100% return last month is probably the very same stock that will tumble (and tumble hard) in the months and years ahead. The same goes for bonds and mutual funds and, potentially, even real estate.

You must take on some risk in order to reap the benefits of investing. That's the bad news. The good news is that sometimes, over time, a decent investment may bounce back and make investors whole again.

What's the best I can hope for?

The best you can hope to achieve with an investment depends on the nature of the investment. Some investments — such as savings accounts and certificates of deposit (CDs) — offer stable, secure returns. Other investments — such as stocks, bonds, and mutual funds — depend entirely on market conditions. A *return* is an investment's performance over time. It's easy to calculate the best-case scenario with vehicles such as savings accounts and CDs. On the other hand, you can never predict with 100% accuracy what kind of return you will get with more volatile investments such as stocks, bonds, and mutual funds.

You can, however, see how these investments have performed in the past. Recent history has many investors believing that the markets can only go up. If you look at returns on some stock investments, you can understand why.

For example, the top-performing stock in 1998, which was an online Web site called Amazon.com, racked up staggering returns of 966% in 1998. If you were lucky enough to invest $1,000 at the end of 1997, your money would have been worth $10,664 a year later. That's probably the best one-year return any investor can ever hope for — and then some.

The next-best-performing 24 stocks in 1998 returned between 164% and 896%. The best-performing stock mutual funds returned well over 70%. In sharp contrast, the best corporate bonds returned more than 15%. Still, if the average stock returns about 10% a year, 1998 was quite a year for many investors.

In fact, the year capped off a decade-long boom for the stock market in which the top-performing stock (Dell Computer Corp.), over the ten-year period from 1988 to 1999, gave investors a very pleasing 79% average annual return. Equally noteworthy, the next best 24 top-performing stocks returned 43% to 69% in the same period.

On average, however, stocks, bonds, and mutual funds don't give investors these kinds of returns. Large company stocks returned only about 18% during the past decade. Corporate bonds gave investors about 10.8% in the same period.

What's the worst-case scenario?

You've heard about the best you can hope for, now what about the worst? The worst performer in 1998 cost investors a frightening 83%. In other words, $1,000 would have been worth just $170 by the end of the year.

You can lose all of your money in an investment if a company declares bankruptcy.

What's a realistic course?

The good news is that if you try to choose your investments carefully — and subsequent chapters of this book give you the tools to do this — you should be able to minimize your losses. Ideally, your losses from any one investment may even be offset by the successes of your other investments.

The emphasis should be on choosing investments carefully, which means that your expectations need to be realistic, too. Stocks have returned an average annual return of about 10% since the 1930s, so aiming for a 15% or 20% return is unrealistic. Corporate bonds returned about 6% in the same time period, so a 12% long-term average annual return from bonds isn't realistic.

Of course, if you're completely uncomfortable with the prospect of losing money, or if you need your money before five years, then investment vehicles such as stocks and bonds aren't for you. You're better off putting your money into safer, more liquid places such as bank accounts, certificates of deposits, and money market accounts, which I talk about in Chapter 2.

Realizing Gains through Compounding

Starting out as a first-time investor doesn't require a whole lot of money, which means that you don't need to wait until you've accumulated a large reserve of ready cash. You may ask: Why the big rush to start investing?

The answer is simple: You want to begin earning *compound interest* as soon as you can. Compound interest is actually the interest you earn on your interest. For example, if you invested $10,000 and earned 10% interest in the next year, your interest income would be $1,000. If you earned 10% again the following year, the $100 you would earn on the $1,000 (in interest you earned in the current year) would be considered compound interest.

Remember

Compounding is a compelling reason to start and keep investing for the long-term because money left untouched reaps the greatest reward from compounding.

Table 1-1 shows you the power of compounding and how quickly even $100 saved or invested each month can grow under different interest rate scenarios.

Table 1-1:   The Beauty of Compound Interest

% Return	5 years	10 years	15 years	20 years	30 years
0%	$6,000	$12,000	$18,000	$24,000	$36,000
5%	$6,829	$15,592	$26,840	$41,275	$83,573
8%	$7,397	$18,417	$34,835	$59,295	$150,030
10%	$7,808	$20,655	$41,792	$76,570	$227,933
12%	$8,247	$23,334	$50,458	$99,915	$352,992

Tip

To determine how many years it will take to double your money as a result of compounding, you can use the *Rule of 72*. Just follow these steps:

1. Determine what interest rate you think your money will earn.

2. Divide 72 by that interest rate.

The number you get is the number of years it will take to double your money.

For example, suppose that you believe you'll earn 8% annually in the coming years. If you divide 72 by 8, you can see that doubling your money will take nine years.

Focusing on a Goal

You can take the first step toward creating your investment plan by asking yourself a simple question: What do I want to accomplish? Actually, this step is your single most important move toward ensuring that your investment plan has a sound foundation. After all, these goals are the reason that you're launching a personal investment plan. So don't shirk off this exercise. Dream away.

Perhaps you've always wanted to travel around the world or build a beach-front chalet. Or maybe you are interested in going back to school or starting your own business. Write down your goals. Your list of goals can serve as a constant reminder that you're on the course to success.

Don't forget the necessities, either. If you have kids who plan to go to college, you need to start preparing for that expenditure now. Your retirement plans fall into this category as well — now is the time to start planning for it.

Table 1-2 gives you a convenient format for writing down your goals. As you fill in Table 1-2, separate your goals into long-, mid-, and short-term time frames based on when you expect or need to achieve the goal. For example:

■ Buying a vacation home or retiring 10 or more years from now is a long-term goal.

■ Sending your child to college in 5 to 10 years is a mid-term goal.

■ Buying a car in the next 1 to 4 years because you know your current model is likely to be on its last legs is a short-term goal.

As you jot down your goals, also write down their costs. Use your best "guesstimate;" or if you're not sure, search the newspaper for, say, the cost of a beach-front home that approximates the one you want to purchase. Leave the "Time and Monthly Investment" category alone for now — that column represents the next step, which I tell you about shortly.

Table 1-2:   My Goals

Time Frame	Cost	Time and Monthly Investment
Short-term:		
Mid-term:		
Long-term:		

Okay, now for the tricky part. How much do you need to invest each month and over what period of time to achieve your goals?

Of course, you need to know an approximate rate of return before you can plan. Your rate of return will differ, depending on the sort of investment you choose. Research can help you accurately estimate your rate of return. (Chapters 2, 3, and 4 tell you how to go about getting this information for different types of investments.)

As an example, Table 1-3 shows you what you need to invest each month to earn $100,000 over different periods of time.

Need $10,000 instead? Divide the monthly investment amount shown in Table 1-3 by 10. Want to save a million dollars instead? Simply multiply the amount by 10.

Table 1-3: **Monthly Investments to Earn $100,000 at Varying Interest Rates**

Years	5%	8%	10%
5	$1,480	$1,350	$1,280
10	$640	$540	$480
15	$370	$290	$240
20	$240	$170	$130

If you're older, in retirement, or just plain more conservative (and like keeping a good bit of your money in accounts or investments that earn less interest), you may want to use a lower estimated interest rate in your calculations to reflect your situation.

If you're investing in another type of asset — real estate, for example — a realtor in your area can tell you the appreciation rate or the annual rate of return for properties in your area. You can use that rate as a gauge to estimate what you're likely to earn in future years.

Tip

For determining how much you need to sock away annually to meet your goals over a specific period of time, using a scientific calculator is easiest.

Starting Your Savings Now

Throughout the rest of this book, I tell you about different types of investments that match your investment goals. To start out with any sort of investment, you need a cash reserve — and the amount varies, depending on your investment choice.

As you're doing your research and deciding which investments match your goals, start putting away $100 a month in an account earmarked for investment. By the time you determine the investing opportunities that best fit your needs, you should be well on your way to affording your investment.

Watching your dollars multiply can serve as motivation in itself: Your investment accounts may become as or more important to you than some of the other expenses that have eaten up your money in the past.

If you're the type who's been saving gobs of cash in a bureau drawer for a long time and now want to start earning real interest, you're one step ahead of the pack. You have the discipline. Now what you need is the knowledge and the tools.

The following chapters give you the tools you need to select investments and create an investment plan to meet all of your goals, including retirement. You also get the information you need to monitor your investments, so you can keep your plan on track.

CHAPTER 2

UNDERSTANDING SAVINGS, MONEY MARKET ACCOUNTS, AND CDS

IN THIS CHAPTER

- Sticking with the tried-and-true: savings accounts
- Finding out about money market accounts
- Discovering certificates of deposit (CDs)

You can choose to be either a financial tortoise or a financial hare. As a financial hare, you can race ahead, spending everything you earn now and have nothing later. Or, as the financial tortoise, you can pace yourself and spend responsibly, knowing that by spending a little less today, you can spend a lot more tomorrow. Assuming that you choose to be a financial tortoise, slowly and steadily socking away savings, where are you going to put those first dollars that you've set aside?

This chapter is about vehicles (investment options) that are appropriate for money that you don't want to put at great risk — for example, money that you have earmarked for emergency funds, or money that you're saving to buy a car, furniture, or a home within the next few years. By keeping your short-term money somewhere safe and convenient, you can feel comfortable putting your long-term money at somewhat greater risk. (Chapters 3 and 4 tell you about these kinds of riskier investments.)

Although they may not be the most exciting investments you'll ever make, savings accounts, money market accounts, and certificates of deposit (CDs) are worthwhile considerations for people who are just starting out. Everyone should have some money in stable, safe investment vehicles. Savings accounts, money market accounts, and CDs are all basic savings tools and are the first step on your path to investing. These tools can help you build up the money that you need in order to start investing in other ways.

As you learn about investment vehicles through this book, you find out which ones are good for short-term investments and which ones are best to go with for the long haul. How you invest your money depends largely on two factors: how long the money can remain out of your reach (time), and how much of it you can afford to lose (risk). Some investments are a lot riskier than others.

In this chapter, I tell you about the safest investments for short-term money that you can't afford to lose, and I also discuss what you need to know before you throw your hard-earned dollars into the pot.

Starting with Savings Accounts

Savings accounts are a form of investment — a very safe form. Although many banks don't pay interest on checking accounts, all banks pay interest on savings accounts.

For the most part, interest rates offered for savings accounts differ only slightly from institution to institution. Prior to the start of banking deregulation in 1986, banks used to pay 5% daily interest on all savings accounts because federal regulation specified that amount. Unfortunately, 5% interest rates on savings accounts are history. Today, the average savings account earns about 2% daily interest.

Look at the bar chart in Figure 2-1 to see how your money fares in a savings account investment with a 2% interest rate and a 3% rate of inflation. Assume that you've made an initial investment of $100 and faithfully add $50 per month for the next five years.

Figure 2-1: Suggested investment goals and uses.

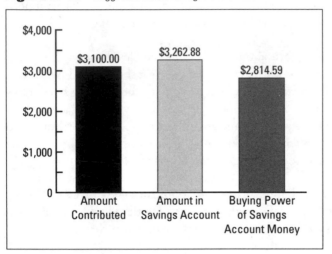

Although the amount in your savings account reaches $3,262.88 — $162.88 more than the amount you actually contributed — the actual buying power of that investment is only $2,814.59, due to the rate of inflation. That's $2,814.59 more than you would have had, had you not committed to socking away some money for the future. But as investments go, you wouldn't want to rely wholeheartedly on a savings account because the return on your investment is so low. Of course, factors such as the interest rate and rate of inflation play a major role in how well your money does in this type of investment vehicle.

Web sites such as www.bankrate.com and financial magazines such as *Money* publish lists of the highest-paying savings accounts each month.

Some banks offer the incentive of earning additional interest on a savings account by using a *tiered account system*. This system enables you to earn higher interest if your account balance is consistently over an amount specified by the bank. This amount is usually at least $1,000, but it may be higher.

Most banks charge a monthly or quarterly maintenance fee for a savings account. Some tack on an additional fee if your balance falls below a required minimum. In addition, you might be required to keep a savings account active for a specified time or face penalties.

What makes savings accounts such a safe investment? If the bank has Federal Deposit Insurance Corporation (FDIC) insurance, your savings account is backed by the full strength and credit of the federal government. If the institution fails, Uncle Sam sees that you get your savings back — up to $100,000. As with any other insurance, you may sleep better knowing that it's there in the worst-case scenario.

Although putting your money in a savings account has serious limitations if it's your one and only investment strategy, having some of your money in a cash reserve makes sense.

Chapter 6 gives you some guidelines for shopping around for a savings account. Make sure that you check out that chapter before calling a bank, savings and loan, or credit union to ask about a savings account.

Seeking Another Safe Haven: Money Market Accounts

Money market accounts and savings accounts are nearly identical, except that money market accounts offer better interest than a savings account. Money market accounts also offer some check-writing privileges. In exchange for these benefits, most institutions require a high minimum balance for money market accounts, averaging between $500 and $2,500.

Don't confuse money market accounts with money market funds. Both money market accounts and money market funds are used to "park" cash and still maintain liquidity. Money market funds, however, are a type of mutual fund. To learn about money market funds, turn to Chapter 3.

Remember

Money market accounts, offered by banks, savings and loans, and credit unions, are a good way to keep money that you may need to get your hands on in a hurry. Money market accounts earn more interest than you would with a savings account without risking a loss in value (which could be the case if you put the same money into stocks and had to turn them into cash quickly). For medium-term expenses, such as saving for a down payment on a car or furniture, a money market account can be a good choice. Money market accounts can also be a good place to put the three months' salary that you set aside for emergencies.

Money market accounts function like a checking account in that you can write a minimum number of checks (usually three) on the account each month. However, in some cases, money market account holders are allowed to make unlimited free deposits and withdrawals from ATMs in their network.

If you only write a couple of checks a month, a money market account might be worth considering. But usually a hefty fee ($10 to $20) is charged if an account holder writes more than the number of checks permitted. Any additional interest a money market account allows you to earn will quickly be chewed up if you have to pay for extra checks.

Some people use a non-interest-bearing checking account for paying regular bills, and then keep their larger reserve in a money market account to gain a higher rate of return. In fact, some financial institutions offer to link a money market account with a checking account, so if your regular checking account doesn't have sufficient funds to cover a check, the institution automatically transfers money from the money market account to the checking account.

Interest rates for money market accounts vary widely and depend on the amount you deposit. When money market accounts were created in 1982, people could earn 10% or more interest on them. During the next 10 years, interest rates for money market accounts bobbed up and down but never got back to the early rates.

When you open an account, you get the prevailing interest rate as set by the bank. Most banks change the rate once a week — every Monday morning, for example — and they give you a phone number to call to check the rate. Your rate may improve if you deposit more funds, but often you have to reach a threshold of $15,000 or $30,000 to see a significant increase in your rate.

Chapter 6 gives you some tips on what to look for if you decide to take the plunge into a money market account.

Investing in Certificates of Deposit

If your savings grow to the point where you have more money than you think you need anytime soon, congratulations! One of the places you can consider depositing some of the balance is a certificate of deposit (CD).

A CD is a receipt for a deposit of funds in a financial institution. Like savings accounts and money market accounts, CDs are investments for security.

With a CD, you agree to lend your money to the financial institution for a number of months or years. You can't touch that money for the specified period of time without being penalized.

Why would a financial institution need you to loan it money? Typically, institutions use the deposits they take in to fund loans or other investments. If an institution primarily issues car loans, for example, it's apt to pay attractive rates to lure money to four-year or five-year CDs, the typical car-loan term.

Generally, the longer you agree to lend your money, the higher the interest rate you receive. The most popular CDs are for six months, one year, two years, three years, four years, or five years. There is no fee for opening a CD.

By depositing the money (a minimum of $500) for the specified amount of time, the financial institution pays you a higher rate of interest than if you put your money in a savings, checking, or money market account that offers immediate access to your money. When your CD matures (comes due), the institution returns your deposit to you, plus interest.

The institution notifies you of your CD's maturation by mail and usually offers the option to roll the CD over into another CD. When your CD matures, you can call your institution to find out the current rates and roll the money into another CD, or transfer your funds into another type of account.

Most institutions give you a grace period, ten days or so, to decide what to do with your money when the CD matures. At an FDIC-insured financial institution, your investment is guaranteed to be there when the CD matures.

Financial advisors say that CDs make the most sense when you know that you can invest your money for one year, after which you'll need the money for some purchase you expect to make. The main reward of investing in CDs is that you know for sure what your return will amount to and can plan around it, because CD rates are usually set for the term of the certificate. Be sure to check on the interest rate terms, though, because some institutions change their rate weekly.

For example, after buying a house in early fall, my friend Mark made plans to have the exterior repainted the following spring (a short-term goal). In October, he received a nice $4,000 bonus from work. Knowing that he might be tempted to spend that money on dinners and CDs (the musical kind), Mark invested that $4,000 in a six-month certificate of deposit with a 4.6% interest rate. When spring rolled around, his CD matured, and he received $4,092. That amount he gained in interest may not sound like a lot, but it's about twice as much as he would have received had he deposited the money in a typical savings account. And it's possibly $92 more than he would have had if he had kept the money in his regular, non-interest-bearing checking account.

See Figure 2-2 to see how much money you can make by buying a Certificate of Deposit versus investing in a savings account.

Warning

The major risk is that interest rates can rise sharply before your CD matures. That situation costs you the opportunity to earn more on your money through some other form of investment.

Figure 2-2: Comparing gains on a CD versus a savings account, with an initial investment of $4,000.

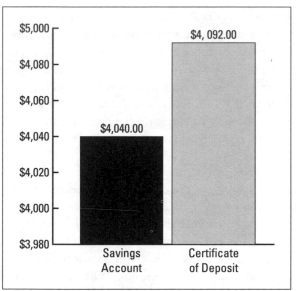

The interest rates paid on CDs are contingent on many factors. In general, they tend to mirror the interest rates in the general market. Most bank CDs are tied to the rates paid on treasury notes and treasury bills. (Treasury rates are the rates offered by the Federal Reserve when they issue treasury obligations.) If the two-year treasury note pays a good rate, interest rates on the bank's CDs tend to be at a good rate, too.

It pays to shop around for CD specials to get the best interest rate. Remember to check out the rates at savings and loans and credit unions. Credit unions typically pay up to half of a percentage point higher interest on CDs, whereas savings and loans generally pay more than banks but less than credit unions.

If you want your money back before the end of the CD's term, you will be heavily penalized, usually with the loss of six months' worth of interest. A second drawback is that CDs are taxable. Whatever interest you earn, you must pay taxes on at both the federal and state levels. However, assuming that you're not in a high tax bracket, the taxes shouldn't be a huge consideration for most people starting out.

If rates are low, you may want to purchase shorter-term CDs and wait for rates to rise. This way, you won't be tying up your funds for long periods of time while rates might be climbing. As another option, some banks might allow you to add money to a CD account at the interest rate of that particular day. The advantage to this method is that if you open the account on a day when the rate is low, you can increase your earnings by adding money at a higher rate, later.

Turn to Chapter 6 for specific information on what questions to ask when shopping around for a CD. See Table 2-1 for some suggested uses for entry-level investments.

Table 2-1:   The Uses for Entry-Level Investments

Type of Investment	Suggested Use
Savings account	Tuck away some money in a savings account to allow you to access it quickly for emergencies, such as car repairs or dentist bills.
Money market account	Money market accounts allow you ready access to your money. Because they offer a higher interest rate than savings accounts, you should consider storing your three-month salary reserve here.
Certificate of Deposit (CD)	CDs are great investments if you are saving for larger ticket items such as a down payment on a car or a major appliance — items you don't intend on purchasing for at least a year.

CHAPTER 3
UNDERSTANDING MUTUAL FUNDS, 401(K)S, AND IRAS

IN THIS CHAPTER

- Finding out about 401(k)s and IRAs
- Mastering mutual funds

The investments that I describe in this chapter do carry some risk — you could lose some or all of your investment money in the worst-case scenario. However, the investments I talk about in this chapter — 401(k)s, Individual Retirement Accounts (IRAs), and mutual funds — are managed by professionals, which reduces the risk somewhat. Read on for the specifics.

Investing in 401(k)s

If you earn employment income from a for-profit company, you may have the option of putting money in a 401(k), a retirement account that appreciates without taxation until you retire or leave the company. (Not all companies sponsor plans, especially small companies, and 401(k)s are not available to state and municipal workers — check with your employer to see if your company offers this plan.)

With a 401(k), the employee contributes pretax salary to the plan. Generally, a 401(k) allows you to contribute a certain percentage of your income each year to the plan.

Companies often match a portion of their employees' contributions to the 401(k). Many employers add 25 cents or even 50 cents more to each dollar an employee chooses to contribute. A typical formula is for an employer to match 50% of what an employee puts in, up to 6% of his or her salary. The plan may also allow an employee to make after-tax contributions.

Money that is contributed to the company's 401(k) is then invested in various, predetermined ways. Many plans typically provide between four and seven investment options, including mutual funds, stocks, and bonds. Usually, a plan offers at least one stock fund, a balanced fund, a bond fund or fixed income account, and maybe a money market account.

Note that individual stocks and bonds are *not* allowed in 401(k) plans. One exception is the company's own stock. For example, General Motors employees can purchase that company's stock in the General Motors 401(k) plan.

The plan lets you decide which investments you want to put your 401(k) money in. You can put all of your contribution into one investment, or you can specify percentages of your contribution to be invested in several of the investment choices. This point is where you can face some risk — it's up to you to decide where to put your money.

Because your contributions to a 401(k) are excluded from your reported income, they are tax-deferred from federal and state income taxes. By using a 401(k), you get an immediate tax deduction for your contribution. A third or more of the average person's 401(k) contribution represents money he or she would have had to pay in federal and state taxes. The beauty of the 401(k) is that the money gets to work for you, rather than the government, in the years ahead. Plus, the money grows over the years without taxation.

If you're not already convinced that a 401(k) can be a great investment, here are some other compelling benefits to consider:

■ Many plans offer an automatic payroll deduction feature. You never miss the money you contribute and payroll deduction makes investing easier.

■ Professionals manage the investment choices in most plans.

■ Most plans allow access to money in an emergency.

■ Account services keep you informed with regular reports. You may even have access to a toll-free number to call for information.

■ Your money can go with you from job to job. Even after you leave your employer, you can roll your retirement money into other tax-deferred retirement accounts, such as an IRA (see the section "Investing in Individual Retirement Accounts" later in this chapter).

Unlike a traditional pension plan (which promises a set dollar figure in benefits when you retire), the amount of money your 401(k) provides upon retirement is determined by how much is invested and the way it grows. The regular account statements you'll receive offer an indication of your likely return, but there's no way to predict how much you'll get until the day you actually retire.

Deciding not to participate because you don't want to cut back on your take-home pay or telling yourself retirement is a long way off may prove to be a big mistake. You risk ending up without enough money after you retire.

Deciding where to put your 401(k) money

Most 401(k) plans offer a variety of investments, including mutual funds, stock funds, and bond funds. Deciding which of these investments to put your money in takes research.

(Chapter 4 tells you all about how to research stocks and bonds, and I tell you more about mutual funds later in this chapter in the section "Defining Mutual Funds.")

You don't have to put all your 401(k) money into one investment vehicle. Unless your research tells you otherwise, you should invest only a certain percentage of your money in a high-risk investment, such as stocks. Also note that most 401(k) plans offer mutual funds whose "risk" ranges from conservative to aggressive.

To determine what percentage of your money to invest in stocks, many financial advisors recommend that you subtract your age from 100. For example, if you're 25, you should have 75% of your 401(k) money in stocks.

Getting out of a 401(k)

When you retire or leave your company, you can leave your 401(k) invested as it is, roll it over into another retirement account (such as an IRA, which I talk about in the section "Investing in Individual Retirement Accounts," later in this chapter), or withdraw it. People usually face some penalties and an income tax liability for withdrawing the money. You can claim funds from the 401(k) without a penalty after age 59½.

When you're in your 20s and 30s, retirement may seem impossibly far off — so far off, in fact, that it's hard to imagine planning for it now. However, start saving for your retirement, and the sooner the better. In 1998, the Social Security Administration estimated that Social Security will provide less than a quarter of the amount you'll need to pay for housing, food, and other living expenses in your retirement. If you want to retire in comfort, you will have to provide for yourself.

Table 3-1 shows how financially beneficial it is to invest in a 401(k) plan as early as possible. The first column shows the number of years before retirement the employee has been investing in a 401(k) plan. The second column shows the accumulated balance at retirement, assuming annual contributions of $4,000 and an 8% annual return on investment.

Table 3-1: Investing Early for Retirement

Number of Years to Retirement	Accumulated Savings at Retirement
40 years	$1,123,124
30 years	$493,383
20 years	$201,691
10 years	$66,581
5 years	$29,343

Investing in Individual Retirement Accounts

An Individual Retirement Account (IRA) is a tax-saving program (established under the Employee Retirement Security Act of 1974) to help Americans invest for retirement. Anyone who earns money by working can contribute up to $2,000 a year, or 100% of your income, whichever is less. If you don't have access to a 401(k) or other retirement plan, or if you've calculated that your current plan won't completely cover your retirement needs, then an IRA can help.

IRAs offer *tax-deferred growth* — you don't pay any tax on it or the money that it earns for you until you withdraw it during retirement.

You set up your IRA on your own with a bank, mutual fund, or brokerage firm. Like a 401(k), you can invest your IRA money in almost anything you can think of, from aggressive growth stocks to conservative savings accounts.

Some financial planners advise that you use your IRA for investments that produce the highest income, such as stocks paying high dividends, because you defer the taxes. Another tactic is to put the IRA funds into riskier high-growth investments, such as stocks or certain types of mutual funds, because you don't touch the funds until retirement and can always switch them to safer investments as you get older.

I suggest investing in an IRA for the following reasons:

- If your employer doesn't offer a 401(k) plan

- If you've calculated that your current retirement plan won't completely cover your estimated retirement needs, consider investing in an IRA — if you qualify

- To invest in high-yield investments — such as stocks paying high dividends — because your investment dollars are tax-deferred

- To invest in higher risk investments, such as stocks and certain mutual funds, if you don't plan to retire for years to come (by doing so you commit to taking the chance of receiving higher gains for your investment dollar)

You can choose from two types of IRAs: traditional IRA and Roth IRA.

The key benefits of traditional IRAs

If you choose a traditional IRA, your contributions may be tax-deductible, while your savings grow and compound tax-deferred until you withdraw them at retirement.

In certain situations, your entire contribution to a traditional IRA can be tax deductible, meaning that you get to subtract the amount that you contribute from your income, reducing the amount of taxes you have to pay overall. The rules for this tax benefit are as follows:

■ If you're single and don't have an employer-sponsored retirement plan, the full $2,000 is deductible on your income tax return.

■ If you're single and covered by an employer-sponsored plan, you can contribute up to $2,000 and deduct the full amount if your annual adjusted gross income is $30,000 or less. (*Annual adjusted gross income* is defined as your gross income, less certain allowed business-related deductions. Deductions include alimony payments, contributions to a Keogh plan, and in some cases, contributions to an IRA.) If your income is between $30,000 and $40,000, the deduction is prorated. If you make more than $40,000, you can contribute, but you get no deduction. These numbers gradually increase to $50,000 for taking the full deduction and to $60,000 for taking no deduction, until the year 2005.

■ If you're married and file your tax returns jointly, you have an employer-sponsored plan, and your annual adjusted gross income is $50,000 or less, you can deduct the full amount. The figure is prorated from $50,000 to $60,000. After $60,000, you can't take any deduction. By 2007, the income allowances will increase to $80,000 for taking the full deduction and $100,000 for taking no deduction.

■ If your spouse doesn't have a retirement plan at work, and you file a joint tax return, the spouse can deduct his or her full $2,000 contribution until your joint income reaches $150,000. After that, the deduction is prorated until your joint income is $160,000, at which time you can't deduct the IRA contribution.

■ Non-income earning spouses can also open IRAs, and the annual contribution for a married couple filing jointly is $4,000 or 100% of earned income, whichever is less, with a $2,000 maximum contribution for each spouse.

Funds generally can't be taken from a traditional IRA before age 59½ without paying a penalty. If you take money out, taxes and a 10% penalty are imposed on the taxable portion of the distribution.

You can make some withdrawals without paying a penalty. Money can be taken penalty-free if you use it for a first-time home purchase or for higher education fees. You can also withdraw penalty-free in the event of death or disability, or if you incur some types of medical expenses.

After you turn age 70½, you are required to take money from your traditional IRA account, either in the form of a lump-sum payout or a little at a time; withdrawing a little at a time allows you to extend the benefit of the tax shelter.

What's new about the Roth IRA

If your income is below $110,000 (single) or $160,000 (married and filing jointly), you can contribute $2,000 a year to a Roth IRA — and this contribution is permitted even if you participate in other pension or profit-sharing plans.

The *Roth IRA,* introduced in 1998, offers the benefit of tax-free withdrawals (if you are 59½ and the account has been held at least five years). If you choose a Roth IRA, your $2,000 contribution comes out of income you've already paid taxes on (that is, earnings). That's very different from the traditional IRA, in which your contribution may come from pretax earnings.

Like a traditional IRA, the funds contributed to a Roth IRA accumulate tax-free. The big difference is that if you are 59½ and have held the Roth IRA for five years, you never pay tax on the money you withdraw. That means that the earnings on the $2,000 you contribute annually are tax-free.

If your income is more than $110,000 and you're single, or if you're married and you and your spouse have a combined income of over $160,000, you're not eligible for a Roth IRA.

Another advantage of the withdrawal requirements of a Roth IRA is that you're not required to take your money out of a Roth IRA when you reach 70½ as you are with traditional IRAs. In fact, you can leave the money and all the earnings to your heirs, if you want to. This allowance enables you to control the timing and the pace of your withdrawals from the account, potentially allowing the funds to stay there, growing tax-free, for more years.

Investors can contribute to both a traditional IRA and a Roth IRA; however, the total contribution to the two accounts can't exceed the $2,000 annual limit. Many financial advisors say that if you are young and in a low tax bracket, you should probably open a Roth IRA and fund it with the full $2,000 every year. For most people, it's not worth debating over the two because only those who have relatively low incomes or no other active retirement plans can take advantage of the deductibility of the traditional IRA.

Use Table 3-2 to help you compare traditional and Roth IRAs and decide which type of IRA is best for you.

Table 3-2:   Comparing Traditional IRAs and Roth IRAs

Feature	Traditional IRA	Roth IRA
Tax deductible contributions	In some cases	None
Penalty-free withdrawals	None at age 59½	
Withdrawals	Required at age 70½	Never required
Income level	No requirement	Must have income under $110,000 if single; $160,000 if married filing jointly
Tax-free earnings	Earnings taxed upon withdrawal	Earnings never taxed
Annual contribution limit		$2,000 $2,000

Defining Mutual Funds

A mutual fund is managed by an investment company that invests (according to the fund's objectives) in stocks, bonds, government securities, short-term money market funds, and other instruments by pooling investors' money.

Mutual funds are sold in shares. Each share of a fund represents an ownership in the fund's underlying securities (the portfolio).

By law, mutual funds must calculate the price of their shares each business day. Investors can sell their shares at any time and receive the current share price, which may be more or less than the price they paid.

When a fund earns money from dividends on the securities it invests in or makes money by selling some of its investments at a profit, the fund distributes the earnings to shareholders. If you're an investor, you may decide to reinvest these distributions automatically in additional fund shares.

A mutual fund investor makes money from the distribution of dividends and capital gains on the fund's investments. A mutual fund shareholder also can potentially make money as the fund's share per share (called *net asset value,* or *NAV*) increases in value.

```
NAV of a mutual fund = Assets
- Liabilities
÷ Number of shares in the fund
```

(*Assets* are the value of all securities in a fund's portfolio; *liabilities* are a fund's expenses.) The NAV of a mutual fund is affected by the share price charges of the securities in the fund's portfolio and any dividend or capital gains distributions to its shareholders.

Unless you're in immediate need of this income, which is taxable, reinvesting this money into additional shares is an excellent way to grow your investments.

Shareholders receive a portion of the distribution of dividends and capital gains, based on the number of shares they own. As a result, an investor who puts $1,000 in a mutual fund gets the same investment performance and return *per dollar* as someone who invests $100,000.

Mutual funds invest in many (sometimes hundreds of) securities at one time, so they are diversified investments. A *diversified portfolio* is one that balances risk by investing in a number of different areas of the stock and/or bond markets. This type of investing attempts to reduce per-share volatility and minimize losses over the long term as markets change. Diversification offsets the risk of putting your eggs in one basket, such as technology funds. (I discuss diversification in greater detail in Chapter 8.)

A stock or bond of any one company represents just a small percentage of a fund's overall portfolio. So even if one of a fund's investments performs poorly, 20 to 150 more investments can shore up the fund's performance. As a result, the poor performance of any one investment isn't likely to have a devastating effect on an entire mutual fund portfolio. That balance doesn't mean, however, that funds don't have inherent risks: You need to carefully select mutual funds to meet your investment goals and risk tolerance.

The performance of certain classes of investments — such as large company growth stocks — can strengthen or weaken a fund's overall investment performance if the fund concentrates its investments within that class. If the overall economy declines, the stock market takes a dive, or a mutual fund manager picks investments with little potential to be profitable, a fund's performance can suffer.

Unfortunately, unless you have a crystal ball, you have no way to predict how a fund will perform, except to look at the security's underlying risk. If a fund has existed long enough to build a track record through ups and downs, you can review its performance during the last stressful market.

Fortunately for all investors, some companies use a statistical measure called *standard deviation,* which measures the volatility in the fund's performance. The larger the swings in a fund's returns, the more likely the fund will slip into negative numbers.

Companies that track funds' standard deviations include Morningstar Mutual Funds and Value Line Inc., which are mutual fund reporting and ranking services whose newsletters are available in most libraries. You can visit their Web sites at www.morningstar.com and www.valueline.com, respectively.

Considering different types of mutual funds

As you prepare to invest in mutual funds, you need to decide which type of funds best suits your goals and tastes. Basically, you have the following four types of mutual funds to consider:

- Stocks funds, which invest in stocks

- Bond funds (also considered income funds), which invest in bonds

- Balanced funds, also called hybrid funds, which invest in both stocks and bonds

- Money market funds, which invest in short-term investments

Table 3-3 gives you a sense of how many dollars investors allocated to different types of mutual funds in 1998.

Each of these groups presents a wide variety of funds with different characteristics from which to choose. To help you further refine your search to match fund investments to your goals, the following lists offer a general look at some different types of funds available.

Table 3-3: Where Mutual Fund Assets Were in 1998

Fund Type	Overall Assets	New Assets
Stock funds	$2.98 trillion	$159 billion
Bond funds	$831 billion	$74 billion
Balanced funds	$365 billion	$16.5 billion
Money market funds	$1.35 trillion	$235 billion

Stock funds include:

- **Aggressive growth funds:** Managers of these funds are forever on the lookout for undiscovered, unheralded companies, including small and undervalued companies. The goal is to get in when the stock is cheap and realize substantial gains as it soars skyward. That dream doesn't always come true. But if you're willing to accept above-average risk, you may reap above-average gains.

- **Growth funds:** These funds are among the mainstays of long-term investing. They own stocks in mostly large- or medium-sized companies whose significant earnings are expected to increase at a faster rate than that of the rest of the market. These growth funds do not typically pay dividends. Several types are available, including large-, medium-, and small-company growth funds.

- **Value funds:** Managers of these funds seek out stocks that are underpriced — selling cheaply, relative to the stock's true value. The fund's manager believes that the market will recognize the stock's true price in the future. Stock price appreciation is long term. These funds don't typically turn in outstanding performance when the stock market is zooming along, but tend to hold their value a good deal more than growth funds when stock prices slide. That's why value funds are generally believed to be good hedges to more growth-oriented mutual funds. These funds come in large-, medium-, and small-company versions.

- **Equity income funds:** These funds were developed to balance investors' desires for current income with some potential for capital appreciation. These fund managers invest mostly in stocks — often blue chip stocks — that pay dividends. They usually make some investments in utility companies, which are also likely to pay dividends.

- **Growth and income funds:** These funds seek both capital appreciation and current income. Growth and income are considered equal investment objectives.

- **International and global funds:** These two funds may sound like the same type of mutual fund, but they're not. *International funds* invest in a portfolio of only non-U.S. stocks (international securities). *Global funds,* also called *world funds,* can also invest in the U.S. stock markets. In fact, during the 1990s, many global funds handed in remarkable performances not because of their international stock-picking prowess, but because they concentrated the bulk of their assets in U.S. stocks. This is a prime example of the importance of understanding how fund managers are investing your money. I talk more about how to make this determination in the next section.

- **Sector funds:** The managers of these funds concentrate their investments in one sector of the economy, such as financial services, real estate, or technology. Although these types of funds may be a good choice after you've already built a portfolio that matches your investment plan, they have greater risk than almost any other type of fund because these funds concentrate their investments in one sector or industry.

If you're uncomfortable with the potential for significant losses, make sure that a sector fund only accounts for a small percentage of your portfolio — say, less than 10%. Remember, however, that if you invest in a balanced portfolio, your other investments should hold their own if only one industry is impacted.

- **Emerging market funds:** The managers of these funds seek out the stocks of underdeveloped countries and economies in Asia, Eastern Europe, and Latin America. Finding undiscovered winners can prove advantageous, but an emerging market fund — also known as an emerging country fund — isn't a recommended mainstay for new investors because of the potential for loss. When these countries and economies suffer economic decline, they can create significant investor losses.

■ **Single-country funds:** As their name implies, the managers of these funds look for the stock winners of one country. Unless you have close relatives running a country somewhere and have firsthand knowledge about that land's economic prospects, you're wise to steer clear of these funds. The reason is simple: They have unmitigated risk from concentration in one area. For example, when Japan's economy declined in 1998, it sent mutual funds that invested exclusively in that country's companies tumbling by more than 50%.

■ **Index funds:** The managers of these funds invest in stocks that mirror the investments tracked by an index such as the Standard & Poors 500. Some of the advantages of investing in index funds include low operating expenses, diversification, and potential tax savings. More than 150 funds, including growth companies, track a variety of different indexes. Although they don't necessarily rely on the performance of any one company or industry to buoy their performance, they do invest in equities that represent a market — such as the U.S. stock market. If and when that market dips, as the U.S. market did by 20% in 1987, index funds can be hit pretty hard.

Bond funds are less risky than stock funds, but also less rewarding. You can choose from the following types of bond funds:

■ Corporate

■ Municipal

■ U.S. Treasury bonds

■ International bond funds

■ Mortgage bond funds

Balanced funds are another investment option. These funds are a mix of stocks and bonds that are also called *blended* or *hybrid funds.* Generally, managers invest in about 60% stocks and 40% bonds. Balanced funds are appealing to investors because even in bear markets, their bond holdings still allow them to pay dividends. (A *bear market* is generally defined as a market in which stock prices drop 20% or more from their previous high.)

Money market funds are arguably the least volatile type of mutual fund. Fund managers invest in things such as short-term bank CDs, U.S. Treasury bills, and short-term corporate debt issued by established and stable companies. This type of mutual fund is ideal for people who may need to use the money to buy something in the short term like a down payment on a home. These funds are also a convenient place to pool money for future investment decisions.

Analyzing mutual funds

As you begin your search for mutual funds, make sure that your performance evaluation produces meaningful results. Performance is important because good, long-term earnings enable you to maximize your investments and ensure that your money is working for you. Gauging future performance is not an exact science.

When you evaluate funds, check out the *Morningstar* and *ValueLine* mutual fund newsletters, both available at the library or online (www.morningstar.com and www.valueline.com). A fund's prospectus, which you can request from a fund's toll-free phone number, also outlines the important features and objectives of the fund.

As an additional check on your selection process, compare all your choice funds before making a final decision; avoid choosing one fund in isolation. A single fund can look spectacular until you discover it trails most of its peers by 10%.

Look for the following information when you select mutual funds:

- **One-, three-, and five-year returns:** These numbers offer information on the fund's past performance. A look at all three can give you a sense of how well a fund fared over time and in relation to similar funds.

- **Year-to-date total returns:** This is a fund's report card for the current year, minus operating and management expenses. The numbers can give you a sense of whether earnings are in line with competing funds, out in front, or trailing.

- **Maximum initial sales charges, commissions, or loads:** Unlike stocks and bonds, mutual funds have built-in operating and management expenses. These expenses are in addition to any commission you may pay to a broker or financial planner to buy a fund. A sales charge on a purchase, sometimes called a *load*, is a charge you pay when you buy shares. You can determine the sales charge (load) on purchases by looking at the fee and expense table in the prospectus. *No-load funds* don't charge sales loads. There are no-load funds in every major fund category. However, even no-load funds have ongoing operating and management expenses.

Go for lower-priced funds or no-load mutual funds, which by definition must have expenses no higher than 0.25%. Load funds can have charges of up to 5.75%. What that means is that you must deduct that 5.75% from any annual performance a fund turns in. If it's 10%, you can expect to earn 4.25% after you pay the load or commission.

■ **Annual expenses:** Also called *annual operating expense ratios (AOERs)*, these costs can sap your performance. Before you settle on one fund, review the numbers on at least a few competitors to determine if the fund's expenses are in line with typical industry charges. In general, the more aggressive a fund, the more expenses it incurs trading investments. Before you invest in a particular fund, be cautious if it has an extremely high AOER compared to that of similar funds.

To develop a sense of how expenses can take a big bite out of earnings over the years, consider this example: A $10,000 investment earns 10% over 40 years with a 1% expense ratio, which yields a return of $302,771. The same investment with a 1.74% expense ratio returns $239,177, or $63,594 less.

■ **Manager's tenure:** Consider how long the current fund manager (or managers) has been managing the fund. If it's only been a year or two, take that into consideration before you invest — the five-year record that caught your eye may have been created by someone who has already moved down the road. Fund managers move around a often. In an ideal world, your funds are handled by managers with staying power.

■ **Portfolio turnover:** This tells you how often a fund manager sells stocks in a the course of a year. Selling stocks is expensive, so high turnover over the long run will probably hurt performance. If two funds appear equal in all other aspects, but one has high turnover and the other low turnover, by all means choose the fund with low turnover.

■ **Underlying fund investments:** For your own sake, take a look at the top five or ten stocks or bonds that a fund is investing in. For example, a growth fund may be getting its rapid appreciation from a high concentration in fairly risky technology stocks, or a global fund may have more than 50% of its holdings in U.S. stocks. Neither of these strategies is a mortal sin if you know about and can live with it. If you can't, keep looking for a fund that matches your goals. Looking at underlying investments not only helps minimize your surprises as markets and economies shift, but also enables you to create a balanced portfolio.

CHAPTER 4
UNDERSTANDING STOCKS, BONDS, AND BEYOND

IN THIS CHAPTER

- Discovering stocks
- Understanding bond basics
- Realizing the potential of real estate

The investments I describe in this chapter carry a great potential for return — but that possibility of return comes at a greater risk to your money. Stocks, bonds, and real estate are investment options whose value fluctuates with the market, meaning that the value of these investments can grow and shrink greatly. However, with the information I give you in this chapter, you will be able to make good educated guesses about how to pursue these investments if you choose to.

Sizing Up Stocks

A *stock* is a piece of paper that signifies that you own part of a company. The market price of a stock is directly related to the profits and the losses of the company. In other words, when the company profits, the worth of your stock increases. When the company falters and its profits decline, so does the worth of your stock.

Investors who buy stock own shares of the company. That's why they're called *shareholders*.

Understanding how stocks work

Companies issue stock to raise money to fund a variety of initiatives, including expansion, the development of new products, the acquisition of other companies, or to pay off debt. In an action called an *initial public offering (IPO)*, a company opens sale of its stock to investors.

An investment banker helps underwrite the public stock offering. By *underwrite*, I mean that the investment banker helps the company determine when to go public and what price the stock should be at that time.

When the stock begins selling, the price can rise or fall from its set price depending on whether investors believe that the stock was fairly and accurately priced. Often, the price of an IPO soars during the first few days of trading, but then can later fall back to earth.

After the IPO, stock prices will continue to fluctuate, based on what investors are willing to accept when they buy or sell the stock. In simple terms, stock prices are a matter of supply and demand. If everyone wants a stock, its price rises, sometimes sharply. If, on the other hand, investors are fearful that, for example, the company's management is faltering and has taken on too much debt to sustain strong growth, they may begin selling in noticeable volume. Mass sales can drive the price down. In addition to specific company issues, the price can drop for other reasons, including bad news for the entire industry or a general downturn in the overall economy.

Remember

Stocks are bought and sold on stock exchanges, such as the New York Stock Exchange, Nasdaq, and the American Stock Exchange. Companies that don't have the cash reserves necessary to be listed on one of the exchanges are traded *over-the-counter,* which means that they receive less scrutiny from analysts and large investors such as mutual fund managers.

In addition, professional analysts who are paid to watch companies and their stocks can give a thumbs-up or a thumbs-down to a stock, which in turn can send stock prices soaring or plummeting. These stock analysts sit in brokerage firms on New York's fabled Wall Street and various cities' Main Streets. The analyst's job is to watch closely the actions of public companies and their managers and the results those actions produce.

By carefully monitoring news about a company's earnings, corporate strategies, new products and services, and legal and regulatory problems and victories, analysts give stocks a *buy*, *sell*, or *hold* rating. Such opinions can have a wide-sweeping impact on the price of a stock, at least in the short-term. Rumblings, real or imagined, can send the price of a stock, or the stock market overall, tumbling downward or soaring skyward.

The price of stock goes up and down — a phenomenon known as *volatility* — but if the news creating the stir is short-term, panic is an overreaction. You don't want to sell a stock when its price is down, only to see it make a miraculous recovery a few days, weeks, or even months down the road.

Smart investors who have done their research and are invested for the longer-term won't be impacted by short-term price dips or panics. Unless of course, you use the opportunity to buy a stock you've already researched and were going to buy anyway. The old adage — buy low, sell high — holds as true today as it did 75 years ago.

How low can stock prices go? In October 1987, stock prices tumbled by 22.6%. This decline meant that the value of a $10,000 investment dropped to $7,740. Many stocks recovered, but some did not.

Remember

You can lose all your money with a stock investment, and that risk is why you need to analyze your choices carefully. The three most basic types of risks associated with stock investments are

■ You may lose money.

■ Your stocks may not perform as well as other, similar stocks.

■ A loss may threaten your financial goals.

Stock investing carries certain risks, but they can be minimized by careful investment selection and by diversification, a technique for building a balanced portfolio, which I investigate more thoroughly in Chapter 8.

Recognizing different types of stock

Companies issue two basic kinds of stock, *common* and *preferred,* and each provides shareholders with different opportunities and rights:

■ **Common stock:** Represents ownership in a company. Companies can pay what are called *dividends* to their shareholders. Dividends are paid out from a company's earnings and can fluctuate with the company's performance. *Note:* Not all companies pay dividends.

Common stock offers no performance guarantees, and although this kind of stock has historically outperformed other types of investments, you can lose your entire investment if a company does poorly enough to wipe out its earnings and reputation into the foreseeable future. Common stock dividends are paid only after the preferred stock dividends are paid.

■ **Preferred stock:** Constitutes ownership shares as well, but this stock differs from common stock in ways that reduce risk to investors, but also limit *upside potential,* or upward trends in stock pricing. Dividends on pre-ferred stock are paid before common stock, so preferred stock may be a better bet for investors who rely on the income from these payments. But the dividend, which is set, is not increased when the company profits, and the price of preferred stock increases more slowly than that of common stock. Also, preferred stock investors stand a better chance of getting their money back if the company declares bankruptcy.

A company's stock is also categorized depending on its per-ceived expected performance. Basically, a company's stock falls into one of two categories: *growth* or *value* (see Table 4-1 for a summary of each).

Table 4-1: The Differences between Growth Stocks and Value Stocks

Investor Characteristics	Pros	Cons
Growth Stocks	Investors anticipate higher profits in return for higher stock prices.	The return on investment can be substantial and prove worth the risk. They are less likely to pay dividends; and if they do, they're typically lower than that of value stocks. Stock prices tend to be affected by negative company news and short-term market changes.
Value Stocks	Investors anticipate that the company will experience a turnaround that will produce higher profits in the future.	It costs fewer investment dollars to buy a dollar of their profits. They may never realize the potential that investors project onto them.

Over time, you're likely to buy a mix of both types of stocks for your portfolio, so knowing the different characteristics of each is important. Understanding growth and value stocks can help you evaluate your options more carefully.

Growth companies are typically organizations with a positive outlook for expansion and, ultimately, stock prices that move upward. Investors looking for growth companies usually are willing to pay a higher price for stocks that have consistently produced higher profits because they're betting the companies will continue to perform well in the future.

Because they use their money to invest in future growth, growth companies are less likely to pay dividends than other, more conservative companies; when they do pay dividends, the amounts tend to be lower. An investor who buys a growth stock believes that, according to analysis of the company's history and statistics, the company is likely to continue to produce strong earnings and is therefore worth its higher price.

The stock of a growth company is, however, somewhat riskier because the price tends to react to negative company news and short-term changes in the market. Also, the company may not continue to produce earnings that are worth its higher price.

In contrast, value stocks are out of favor, left on the shelf by investors who are busy reaching for more expensive and trendier items. For that reason, you spend fewer dollars to buy a dollar of their profits than if you invest in a growth stock. When investors buy value stocks, they're betting that they're actually buying a turn-around-story — with a happy ending down the road.

Value companies carry risk, too, because they may never reach what investors believe is their true potential. Optimism doesn't always pay off in profits.

Identifying potential stock investments

What do you need to know to determine which stocks are potential investments? To get started, stick with stocks relating to your own interests or knowledge. If you frequent particular stores or restaurants and you use and like their products, find out if they are publicly held companies. Start identifying and watching these stocks. That advice doesn't mean that you should buy their stock right away. You still have some homework to do.

The following list tells you what to look for when investigating potential stock investments. S&P's *Personal Wealth* newsletter, which is available at most libraries (and online at www.personalwealth.com), along with the *ValueLine* newsletter (www.valueline.com) and any brokerage firm analyst report can provide you with much or all of the following pertinent facts and measures (see Chapter 7 for more information on working with brokerages):

■ **Find out if the industry is growing.** Some industries aren't. News stories on the industry in question can tell you the state of the industry and so can the company's annual report.

Company shareholder departments and the Securities and Exchange Commission (SEC), the Washington, D.C.-based regulator that oversees public companies, can provide you with copies of annual reports and the quarterly reports (called 10Qs) that companies must file. You can also find them on the Internet at www.freeedgar.com.

■ **Find primary competitors.** Don't look at a stock in isolation. A company that looks enticing by itself may look like a 100-pound weakling when you evaluate its strengths and weaknesses next to the leading competitors in the industry. Check out at least two competitors of any stock you're evaluating.

■ **Check out annual earnings and sales.** This is key in deciphering how quickly a company is growing over one-year, three-year, and five-year time periods, and whether its earnings are keeping pace with sales. Look for growth rates of at least 10%.

■ **Look at the stock's price-to-earnings (P/E) ratios.** This is the primary means of evaluating a stock. The *P/E ratio* is derived by dividing a stock's share price by its earnings-per-share. The result tells you how much investors are willing to pay for each $1 of earnings. Those stocks that have faster earnings growth rates also tend to carry higher P/Es, which means that investors are willing to pay through the nose to own shares. The value of a P/E ratio, however, can be subjective. One investor may think that a particular company's P/E ratio of 20 is high, while another may consider it low to moderate.

■ **Find out the price-to-book value (P/B) ratio.** The *P/B ratio* is the stock's share price divided by *book value,* or a firm's assets minus its liabilities. This ratio is a good comparison tool and can tell you which companies are asset-rich and which are carrying more debt.

A low P/B ratio can be an indicator that a stock may be a good value investment.

■ **Check out the stock's price-to-growth flow ratio.** This ratio is the share price divided by *growth flow* (annual earnings plus research-and-development costs) per share. This is a useful measure for assessing fast-moving companies, especially in the technology sector, where management often puts profits back into product development.

■ **Look at the stock's PEG ratio.** The *PEG ratio* is a company's P/E ratio divided by its expected earnings' growth rate and is an indicator of well-priced stock.

In a soaring stock market, like the one that dominated the 1990s, a PEG ratio below 1.5 suggests that a stock may be a good value. A PEG ratio above 2 can indicate that a stock may be overheated.

■ **Look ahead.** Projections of five-year annual growth rates and five-year P/E ratios can tell you whether analysts believe that the companies you're evaluating can continue to grow at their current rate, can beat it, or will start to fall behind.

Make a list of the stocks you are interested in and watch their performance over time. Doing so gives you a feel for how the stocks respond to different types of economic and market news. You can also see which stocks' prices move around and are more volatile.

So does your own analysis indicate that you have a winner on your hands or a dog? If you're unsure, sit tight and watch what happens in the weeks and months ahead. Watching several stocks over a period of time not only tells you how well they're doing, or not doing, it can also show you how well you're honing your own stock analysis skills.

Chapter 7 tells you about how to purchase a stock after doing your research.

Learning about Bond Basics

A bond is basically an IOU. When you purchase a bond, you are lending money to a government, municipality, corporation, federal agency, or other entity. In return for the loan, the entity promises to pay you a specified rate of interest during the life of the bond and to repay the *face value* of the bond (the *principal* you invested) when it *matures* or comes due.

The entity to whom you're lending money when you buy a bond is called the *issuer.*

Bonds aren't like stocks. You are not buying part ownership in a company or government when you purchase a bond. Instead, what you're actually buying — or betting on — is the issuer's ability to pay you back with interest.

Understanding how bonds work

You have a number of important variables to consider when you invest in bonds, including the stability of the issuer, the bond's maturity or due date, interest rate, price, yield, tax status, and risk. As with any investment, ensuring that all these variables match up with your own investment goals is key to making the right choice for your money.

Be sure to buy a bond with a maturity date that tracks with your financial plans. For instance, if you have a child's college education to fund 15 years from now and you want to invest part of his or her college fund in bonds, you need to select vehicles that have maturities that match that need. If you have to sell a bond before its due date, you receive the prevailing market price, which may be more or less than the price you paid.

In general, because they often specify the yield you'll be paid, bonds can't make you a millionaire overnight like a stock can. What can you expect to earn? Long-term corporate bonds, for example, have paid anywhere from an average of 1% in the 1950s to 13% in the 1980s, when in general all bonds did well. What can you expect to lose? That depends on how safe the issuer is. You can read more about this issue in Chapter 5.

Recognizing different types of bonds

Bonds come in all shapes and sizes, and they enable you to choose one that meet your needs in terms of your investment time horizon, risk profile, and income needs. First, here is a look at the different types of U.S. government securities that are available:

■ **Treasury bills:** T-Bills: T-Bills have a minimum purchase price of $10,000 and are offered in 3-month, 6-month, and 12-month maturities. T-Bills do not pay current interest, but instead are always sold at a discount price, which is lower than par value. The difference between the discount price and the par value received is considered interest. For example, if you pay the discount price of $9,500 for a $10,000 T-Bill, you pay 5% less than you actually get back when the bill matures. Par is considered to be $10,000.

■ **Treasury notes:** Treasury notes have maturities of 2 to 10 years. The minimum investment is $1,000, but they are also issued in $5,000 and $10,000 amounts. Treasury notes have coupons that pay interest every six months.

■ **Treasury bonds:** With maturities of up to 30 years, these are the long-term offerings from the Treasury Department; as such, these bonds typically pay the highest interest. The minimum investment is $1,000, but they are also issued in $5,000 and $10,000 amounts. Treasury bonds have coupons that pay interest every six months.

■ **Zero-coupon bonds:** Zero-coupon bonds do not pay current interest. You buy the bond at a steep discount, and interest accrues (builds up) during the life of the bond. At maturity, the investor receives all the accrued interest plus his/her original investment. Zero-coupon bonds are taxed each year on the interest earned (even though it's not actually paid out), unless it is a zero-coupon municipal bond (which would be free of federal and possibly state taxes.) Zero-coupon bonds are usually used in IRA accounts.

- **Savings bonds:** These have been the apple pie of American investing for years. They act like zero coupon bonds, but you can purchase them in small denominations from banks or the Treasury Department. For more zest, the agency began offering inflation-indexed bonds in 1998, which guarantee that your return will outpace inflation. The bond's yield is actually based on the inflation rate plus a fixed rate of return, such as 3%. Interest on savings bonds is not taxed until the bond is cashed in.

Financial experts generally see United States government bonds as the safest investment bet around. But remember that risk and reward are tradeoffs that you need to look at in tandem. As with all investments, the safer the investment, the less you're likely to earn or lose!

The following are other types of available bonds:

- **Municipal bonds:** These are loans you make to a local government, whether it's in your city, town, or state. Because most are free from local (if you live in the municipality issuing the bond), state (if the municipality issuing the bond is in your state of residence), and federal taxes, they can be valuable to those who seek tax relief — often folks in higher income tax brackets. Generally, these bonds have proven their worth as safe investments over the years (although there have been a few instances when municipalities proved unreliable); they pay a stated interest rate over the life of the bond. Some municipal bonds are insured, making them safe from default. Municipal bonds are generally available at minimums of $5,000.

- **Corporate bonds:** These are issued by companies that need to raise money, including public utilities and

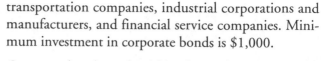

transportation companies, industrial corporations and manufacturers, and financial service companies. Minimum investment in corporate bonds is $1,000.

Corporate bonds can be riskier than either U.S. government bonds or municipal bonds because companies can go bankrupt. So a company's credit risk is an important tool for evaluating the safety of a corporate bond. Even if an organization doesn't throw in the towel, its risk factor can be enough to cause agency analysts, such as Standard & Poors or Moody's, to downgrade the company's overall rating. If that happens, you may find it more difficult to sell the bond early.

- **Junk bonds:** Junk bonds pay high yields because the issuer may be in financial trouble, have a poor credit rating, and are likely to have a difficult time finding buyers for their issues. Although you may decide that junk bonds or junk bond mutual funds have a place in your portfolio, make sure that spot is small because these bonds carry high risk.

Although junk bonds may look particularly attractive at times, think twice before you buy. They don't call them junk for nothing. You could potentially suffer a total loss if the issuer declares bankruptcy. As one wag suggested, if you really believe in the company so much, invest in its stock, which has unlimited upside potential.

Identifying potential bond investments

Here's a look at some items you need to evaluate before investing in a fund:

- **Issuer stability:** This is also known as *credit quality,* which assesses an issuer's ability to pay back its debts, including the interest and principal it owes its bond holders, in full and on time. Although many corporations, the United States government, and a multitude of municipalities have never defaulted on a bond, you can expect that some issuers can and will be unable to repay. (Chapter 5 tells you more about assessing issuer stability.)

■ **Maturity:** A bond's maturity refers to the specific future date when you can expect your principal to be repaid. Bond maturities can range from as short as one day all the up to 30 years. Make sure that the bond you select has a maturity date that works with your needs. T-Bills and zero coupon bonds pay interest at maturity. All other bonds pay interest every six months. Most investors buy bonds in order to have a steady flow of income (from interest).

Warning

The longer the maturity in a bond, the more risk associated with it — that is, the greater the fluctuation in bond value based upon changes in interest rates.

■ **Interest rate:** Bonds pay interest that can be fixed-rate, floating, or payable at maturity. Most bond rates are fixed until maturity, and the amount is based on a percentage of the face or principal amount.

■ **Face value:** This is the stated value of a bond. The bond is selling at a *premium* when the price is above its face value; pricing below its face value means that it's selling at a *discount*.

■ **Price:** The price you pay for a bond is based on an array of different factors, including current interest rates, supply and demand, and maturity.

■ **Current yield:** This is the annual percentage rate of return earned on a bond. You can find a bond's current yield by dividing the bond's interest payment by its purchase price. For example, if you bought a bond at $900 and its interest rate is 8% (0.08), the current yield is 8.89% — 8% or 0.08 ÷ $900 = 8.89.

■ **Yield to maturity (YTM):** This tells you the total return you can expect to receive if you hold a bond until it matures. Its calculation takes into account the bond's face value, its current price, and the years left until the bond matures. The calculation is an elaborate one, but the broker you're buying a bond from should be able to give you its YTM. The YTM also enables you to compare bonds with different maturities and yields.

Don't buy a bond on current yield alone. Ask the bank or brokerage firm from whom you're buying the bond to provide a YTM figure so that you can have a clear idea about the bond's real value to your portfolio.

■ **Tax status:** The interest you earn on U.S. Treasury bills, notes, and bonds is exempt from local and state tax. Interest paid on municipal bonds is usually exempt from local (if you live in the municipality issuing the bond), state (if the municipality issuing the bond is in your state of residence), and federal tax, although you pay capital gains tax on any increase in the price of the bond. On corporate bonds, you pay both state and federal taxes, where applicable, for interest paid and capital gains taxes on any increase in price.

If you sell a corporate, treasury, or municipal bond for more than you paid for it, you'll pay capital gains tax on the difference. Turn to Chapter 7 to find out how to purchase a bond, if you are so inclined.

Investing in Real Estate

There are three ways that you can become a real estate investor: first, by buying your own home; second, by buying an investment property; and third, by investing in a real estate investment trust (REIT).

Although it's true that over time, real estate owners and investors have enjoyed rates of return comparable to the stock market, real estate is not a simple way to get wealthy. Nor is it for the faint of heart or the passive investor. Real estate goes through good and bad performance periods, and most people who make money in real estate do so because they invest over many years.

Buying your own home

Most people invest in real estate by becoming homeowners. Part of the American dream is that the *equity*, which is the difference between the market value of your home and the loan owed on it, increases over time to produce a significant part of your net worth.

Unless you have the good fortune to live in a rent-controlled apartment, owning a home should be less expensive than renting a comparable home throughout your adult life. Why? As a renter, your housing costs will follow the level of inflation, while as a homeowner, the bulk of your housing costs are not exposed to inflation if you have a fixed-rate mortgage.

Figure 4-1 illustrates the difference in expenditure when comparing owning and renting a home. In this graph, I assume that the homeowner has a 30-year, fixed-rate mortgage of 7.5% on $150,000, and the renter starts out with an $800 per month rent payment with annual increases of 4%.

Figure 4-1 shows that at the end of 30 years the renter has paid over $500,000, while the owner has paid less than $375,000. What's more, the owner has increased her equity, also called *net worth*. Owning your home can add to your sense of financial security as the economy fluctuates. In addition to the financial benefits, home ownership gives you more control over your own living space; for example, it allows you more freedom to decorate your home's exterior and interior

Figure 4-1: The expense of owning versus renting your home.

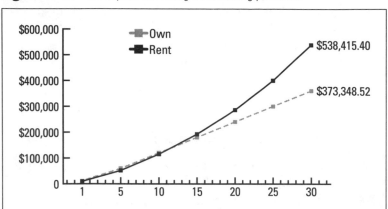

according to your own tastes. Uncle Sam gives homeowners another major financial boost by making your mortgage interest and property tax costs deductible. Although you don't get any tax benefit if you have to sell your home at a loss, any profit made when you sell your primary residence is tax-free up to $250,000 ($500,000 for a married couple) as long as you lived there for at least two of the five years prior to the sale.

Buying an investment property

A second way to invest in real estate is to buy residential housing such as single family homes or multi-unit buildings, and rent them. In many ways, buying real estate in this way isn't an investment, it's a business. Maintaining a property can easily turn into a part-time job. If you're a person who dreams of putting heart and soul into a property, however, it may be worth investigating. If you do decide to take this route, first, be sure that you have sufficient time to devote to the project. Second, be careful not to sacrifice contributions to tax-deductible retirement accounts such as 401(k)s or IRAs in order to own investment real estate.

Remember

Deciding to become a real estate investor depends mostly on you and your situation. Is real estate something that you have an affinity for? Do you know a lot about houses, or have a knack for spotting up-and-coming areas? Are you cut out to handle the responsibilities that come with being a landlord? Do you have the time to manage your property?

Another drawback to real estate investment is that you earn no tax benefits while you're accumulating your down payment. Retirement accounts such as 401(k)s and IRAs (see Chapter 3) may give you an immediate tax deduction as you contribute money to them. If you haven't exhausted your contributions to these accounts, consider doing so before taking a look at investment real estate.

Investing in a real estate investment trust (REIT)

If you don't want to be a landlord, you might consider option number three: investing in real estate through a REIT (real estate investment trust). REITs are diversified real estate investment companies that purchase and manage rental real estate for investors. A typical REIT invests in different types of property, such as shopping centers, apartments, and other rental buildings. You can invest in REITs either through purchasing them directly on the major stock exchanges or through a real estate mutual fund that invests in numerous REITs.

CHAPTER 5

MAKING GOOD FIRST STEPS IN THE MARKET

IN THIS CHAPTER

- Starting out with mutual fund investing
- Beginning to invest in the stock market
- Exploring possibilities in the bond market

Everyone wants a great portfolio of investments, but where do you start? Like any other journey, you begin with that unceremonious first step. If you make the move, you can be on your way to financial comfort and freedom. Sit around for a few more years thinking about what you should be doing, and you'll be that much further behind.

Of course, picking your first investment is not something to do rashly. View your investments as long-term commitments. Don't impulsively make a purchase, thinking that you can change your mind later. Many financial experts recommend a simple approach: Buy one bond fund, one international stock mutual fund, one money market fund, and one U.S. stock mutual fund. And then have confidence in your decision.

First Steps in Mutual Fund Investing

Mutual funds can be a great fit for a first-time investor. Because they're managed by a professional, you don't have to wrack your brain about what individual stock or bond to buy or when to buy it or sell it. At the same time, you get a fairly diversified portfolio in one fell swoop, which involves much less risk than if you invest in only one stock.

If you're uncomfortable with the kind of risk that stocks present, find a good mutual fund for your launch into investing. Starting out with a mutual fund doesn't represent the end of your quest; it's the beginning. You can always select a handful of decent stocks down the road to add to your portfolio.

With more than 8,000 mutual funds to choose from, the world may be your oyster, but you eventually have to make selections that suit you best. In the next three sections, I talk about three types of mutual funds that can be good first investments.

Make sure that you check out a Morningstar or Value Line report on each fund you're considering; one-, three-, five- and ten-year performance track records can yield valuable information. You want to see consistent returns over time and relatively low expenses (ideally 1% or less). If you read the report carefully, you can also get a sense of how a manager approaches his or her investments, and whether the style is more aggressive than you're comfortable dealing with. (See Chapter 3 for more tips on what to look for as you shop for mutual funds.)

Also review the fund's prospectus, which outlines the fund's investment objectives and policies, expenses, and risks. Some better mutual fund companies are starting to graphically depict the worst quarter and year they've experienced, along with the best, so that you can quickly get an idea of how low and high the fund may go with your money.

Balanced funds

Although managers of balanced funds invest to earn respectable returns, they manage first and foremost to avoid sizeable losses. To do this, many invest in bonds. In some fund portfolios, bonds account for as much as 30% or more of the balanced fund's holdings.

Balanced funds seek income and capital preservation as their goal, so they offer moderate capital appreciation as compared to growth funds. Balanced funds don't take as hard a hit as more aggressive funds when the market dips.

Large U.S. growth funds

Large U.S. growth fund managers look for large and mid-size U.S. companies that are fairly stable performers, but have the potential to continue growing. Changes in society, such as the aging of the Baby Boom generation, may be one reason that some companies have good growth potential. For example, some managers like companies in health care, entertainment, travel, and financial services because they have the potential to benefit from the dollars of older, richer Boomers.

A large-company growth index fund

A manager of an index fund invests in companies whose stocks are listed in an index such as the Standard & Poors 500. The fund tracks the performance of the index. The S&P has been the index with the best performance in the past decade. (See Chapter 8 for details on the S&P.) If you want even more diversification, try a fund that invests, for example, in the Wilshire 5000, which tracks all of the stocks listed in the American Stock Exchange, the New York Stock Exchange, and Nasdaq.

Rather than trying to predict the direction of the market, the index funds are designed to match the performance of the index. These funds are considered to be unmanaged because they invest and hold the same stocks as in the index.

Unfortunately, the fact that index funds match the performance of the index is the worst part, too, because in a bear market (when stock prices drop significantly), index funds have no place else to turn for investments but to the index.

Remember, however, that index funds can offer the investor long-term, steady growth.

You can pick a small-company mutual fund, a medium-company mutual fund, a bond mutual fund, and an international mutual fund as you continue building your portfolio, but it's a good idea to start with a fund that invests in large company stocks. Because, since the late 1920s, these types of stock have historical average annual returns of more than 11%, this type of fund can anchor the rest of your portfolio.

Table 5-1 shows a concise view of the characteristics that differentiate these three types of mutual funds.

Table 5-1: Mutual Fund Characteristics

Balanced funds	Most conservative of the stock mutual funds. Fund managers are first and foremost concerned with avoiding big losses; then they concentrate on getting respectable returns.
Large U.S. growth funds	Fund managers invest in large and mid-size U.S. companies that have shown stable returns but have the potential to continue growing.
Large-company growth index funds	Returns match the index's performance and don't rely on the picks of fund managers.

The minimum fund investment

Do you think that you need a fortune to get started? You're wrong. Many fund companies have a $250 minimum investment requirement. Others with $2,500 or $10,000 minimum investments waive those requirements if you're willing to invest $50 or $100 each month or even each quarter.

Individual Retirement Accounts are another way to steer around high minimum investment requirements because many mutual fund companies allow you to start an IRA with $1,000. (A few companies accept $250 as a minimum, but that is becoming more rare.) Almost all mutual funds offer this service to investors in an attempt to capture assets that the funds hope to hold on to for years — until the investors retire. Make sure, however, that you really can use an IRA and aren't just looking for a way into a fund. You can't tap the money until you reach age 59 ½ without paying income taxes and a 10% penalty. If you're investing for retirement, fine. If you're investing to pay for your child's college tuition or a beach house and expect to require the funds well before age 59 ½, find a fund that fits your needs.

First Steps in Stock Investing

If you're willing to roll up your sleeves and do the research necessary to invest in individual companies, a stock may be a good fit for your new portfolio. The key is to avoid excessive risk. The best way to minimize risk is to buy a solid company — one that is essentially a blue chip or a larger-company growth stock. Look for a stock with consistent performance that appears to sustain and even increase over time.

The Dow Jones Industrial Average is the index of blue chips, listing the likes of IBM, Kodak, McDonald's, and Sears. (See Chapter 8 for deatils on the Dow Jones.) These stocks tend to hedge investors' first exposure to equity investing by paying dividends that offset any lackluster performance.

You may also want to seek out a *value stock* — a stock that has been underperforming its peers, but that seems poised to turn things around. An index called "Dogs of the Dow," which is compiled by Dow Jones and printed in *The Wall Street Journal,* lists specifically those stocks that are on the outs. Of course, none is guaranteed to become the next best stock to own. You have to judge for yourself by looking at a company's long-term growth and earnings; its price-to-earnings (P/E) ratio; and any company news that can give you insight into debt level, acquisitions on the horizon, and competitive edge of products, services, and management. (The P/E ratio is derived by dividing a stock's share price by its earnings-per-share price. The result shows how much investors are willing to pay for each $1 of earnings — see Chapter 4 for details.)

Annual reports, which you can request from a company's own investor relations department, can give you some of these details; but for the rest, you have to sift through analysts' reports and check the charts that are available from firms such as Morningstar (www.morningstar.com) and Standard & Poors (www.stockinfo.standardpoor.com). These services can show you a stock's ups and downs over the years and even over the past month. Analysts' reports can project a company's earnings, dividends, and price growth over the next few months and years.

Don't forget to check on competitors, too. Because all performance data is relative, a company that may seem like a great catch may actually be inferior to its peers, but you won't know that if you don't check. For example, if you're thinking about investing in McDonald's, make sure that you check out the stocks for Wendy's, too.

First Steps in Bond Investment

If you're in or near retirement and consider safety, or reduced risk, a priority, you can buy a bond. Corporate bonds are sold in increments of $1,000, and municipal bonds (tax-free) in increments of $5,000.

Before you buy a bond, determine how long you want to hold the bond, which tells you what maturity date you're after; how safe the bond you want to own must be; and how much interest (yield) you need.

Tip

Short-term U.S. government bonds are the safest, but highly rated municipal bonds and corporate bonds can be almost as safe. To determine if the extra risk is warranted, compare the rates paid by the bonds you're considering with the rates paid by treasury bills. Because Treasury bills are the safest investment, if other bonds aren't paying much more, there may be little reason to take on the additional risk.

If you're not sure, comparison-shop. If a bond isn't issued by the U.S. government, check the issuer's financial position by its quality rating with Moody's or Standard & Poors. Table 5-2 shows the rating system these agencies use. Stick with a bond with a rating of A or above.

Table 5-2:   Credit Ratings

Credit Risk Score	Moody's	Standard & Poors
Highest quality	Aaa	AAA
High quality	Aa	AA
Upper medium	A	A
Medium grade	Baa	BBB
Lower medium	Ba	BB
Speculative	B	B
Poor quality	Caa	CCC
Most speculative	Ca	CC
No interest paid or has filed for bankruptcy	C	C
In default	C	D

Can a bond issuer meet its bond and other debt obligations on time, in full? That's the question that is analyzed closely by rating agencies such as Standard & Poors and Moody's Investors Service. Before buying a bond, checking a bond's rating should become a routine part of any purchase. Ask the broker or bank you're buying from to see the rating.

The consensus, especially for beginning investors, is to steer clear of anything not rated A or above by Standard & Poors or Moody's.

Be sure to find out how low the bonds or underlying bond investments have dipped in terms of performance over the years. You can then gauge your own exposure, although if you hold a bond until maturity, the mountains and valleys of performance don't matter.

If you're buying a government bond or bond fund, you may also want to consider whether you want taxable or nontaxable investments. This decision depends on your tax bracket and your perspective regarding how much you plan to invest and earn over the years.

The Don'ts of First-Time Investing in Mutual Funds, Stocks, and Bonds

No one wants you to become so overwhelmed by the prospect of the seemingly endless investment choices that you hesitate to start. At the same time, before you get carried away, here are a few wise words that may help protect you as you set out to achieve your investment goals.

Don't invest for the short-term

Plan to invest only what you can afford to tuck away for years. Even if the stock market crashes the day after you buy your first investment, you stand a much better chance of recovering your dollars if you have five or more years to stay invested, instead of having to cash in investments next month or next year.

Don't play with fire

Avoid speculative, risky investments, especially those whose terms and properties you can't understand no matter how many times a broker or friend explains them. Your comfort level is important, so remember that some of the best investment options can seem boring and mundane.

Risky investments include those based on premises that seem farfetched, such as an underwater casino, or those that promise unbelievable returns. They may also have terms that are unfavorable, such as an investment that gives a company or other investors the right to buy you out at the price you paid if the investment turns profitable.

If an investment seems too good to be true, it is.

Don't put all your eggs in one basket

Just because one type of investment is doing well this month or this year doesn't mean that its success will continue or that you should invest all your money in that arena. Also, you don't want to scare yourself out of continued investing by choosing a highly volatile investment that may start losing your dollars immediately.

Don't forget to do your homework

Wise investing relies on research, which can be hard work. Just because someone touts an investment in an Internet chat room or across the lunch table at work doesn't mean it's a good buy. Do your homework. If you wouldn't buy an investment except for the go-go advice, don't buy it.

CHAPTER 6

TAKING THE PLUNGE INTO SELF-SERVE INVESTMENTS

IN THIS CHAPTER

- Shopping for savings accounts
- Making your mark with money market accounts
- Knowing what to ask about CDs

I talk about the basics of self-serve investments — including savings accounts, money market accounts, and CDs — in Chapter 2. When it's time to roll up your sleeves and actually get your money invested in these vehicles, this chapter tells you how to take the plunge.

Diving into Savings Accounts

Rather than "taking the plunge," opening a savings account is more like dipping your toe into the water. But, we've all got to start somewhere, and this is where many people start out. Opening a savings account can be the first step to a lifetime of good savings habits.

You've probably heard the advice, "Pay yourself first." That doesn't mean give yourself some cash so that you can go shopping. When you sit down to pay bills, write the first check to a savings or investment account. It doesn't matter if you start with a very small amount, just make savings a habit. And when you get bonuses and raises, you can increase those checks you write to yourself.

When you shop for a bank, savings and loan, or credit union where you can open a savings account, make sure to ask the following questions:

- **Is there a required minimum balance for a savings account?** Some institutions charge a fee if your balance falls below a required minimum.

- **What are your fees for savings accounts?** You can expect to be charged either a monthly or quarterly maintenance fee. The institution may also charge you a fee if you close the account before a specified period of time.

- **How much interest will I get on my savings?** Expect around 2% interest.

- **Is the account federally insured?** Ask specifically whether the institution has Federal Deposit Insurance Corporation (FDIC) insurance. If it does, then you can get up to $100,000 of your savings back if the bank fails.

- **What services do you offer?** Many banks now offer banking by telephone or the Internet.

- **Does the bank use a tiered account system?** A tiered account system allows you to earn higher interest if your account balance is consistently over an amount specified by the bank.

Call around to at least three different institutions (banks, savings and loans, and/or credit unions) to compare their offerings. (You can also call brokerage firms, which offer CDs, to find out what their minimums and fees are.)

If the answers to all of these questions come out about equal, choose the institution that's most convenient for you and offers the best service, convenient hours, friendly tellers — whatever suits your banking habits best.

Shopping for Money Market Accounts

When you open a money market account, as the song says, you'd better shop around. On any given day, certain banks may try to attract deposits. Those banks often offer money market accounts that yield over 5%, although the average yield nationwide is more in the range of 2.5%. In many cases, the yield also depends on the amount you deposit.

The first step in opening a money market account is to decide which type best suits your needs. Money market accounts come in three types:

- **The basic money market account:** These usually require a minimum opening deposit of $100.

- **The "tiered" money market account:** These often require a minimum opening deposit in excess of $100 and pay a higher yield than most basic accounts. For example, you might earn 2.5% interest with a $500 account balance, but as much as 5% interest or more with a balance of $50,000.

- **The package deal:** This is a money market account coupled with a savings account, certificates of deposit, and other bank investments. Because the package deal utilizes several products, banks and credit unions may offer a slightly higher yield than they do for basic or tiered accounts. What's more, the minimum deposit may be waived.

When you're in front of your friendly neighborhood bank representative, ask the questions contained in the worksheet in Table 6-1. Shop around to at least three different institutions before you commit your money.

Table 6-1: Shopping for a Money Market Account

	Name of Institution #1:	Name of Institution #2:	Name of Institution #3:
Questions to Ask:			
Is there more than one version of a money market account? If so, what are the differences?			
Is there a minimum deposit to open an account?			
What is the interest rate paid on the account?			
Do yields improve if my balance grows?			
If so, do I earn higher yields on the entire balance or only part of it?			
Is there a monthly maintenance fee?			
If so, is there any way to avoid that fee?			
Is there a fee if my balance drops below the minimum?			
Would the institution consider waiving the fees if I open other accounts here, such as a savings account?			
What's the fee for writing more than three checks a month on the account?			
What's the fee for using automated teller machines?			

Comparing CDs

When you shop around for a CD, ask the following questions. As with the other investments I discuss in this chapter, talk to at least three different institutions before you take the plunge.

- **What's the minimum deposit to open the account?** Usually this amount is $500.

- **What's the interest rate? What is the compounded annual yield?** Interest is the percent that the bank pays you for your allowing them to keep your money. The rate of interest is also called *yield*. Compounded annual yield comes into play if a bank is paying interest monthly, for example. Once the first month's interest is credited to your account, that interest starts earning interest, too, meaning that the compounded annual yield is slightly higher than the interest rate.

- **How often is the interest compounded?** Remember, the more frequently it's compounded, the better it is for you. Continuous compounding is best.

- **Is the interest rate fixed or variable?** Make sure that the institution offers you a way to get current interest rates quickly and easily — by phone, for example.

- **Can you add to your fund at a higher interest rate if the rate goes up while your money is invested?** If the rate goes up substantially, and you can add to your fund, then you can significantly increase your yield.

- **What's the penalty for early withdrawal?** These penalties can wipe out any interest you earn.

- **What happens to the deposit when the CD matures?** Does the institution roll a matured CD into a new one of a similar term? Does it mail a check? Credit your checking account?

CHAPTER 7

TAKING THE PLUNGE INTO BROKERAGE INVESTMENTS

In Chapter 4, I offer a short course on the basics of stocks and bonds, the different kinds of securities in each of these broad categories, and the way these instruments fit into an investment plan.

When it comes time to actually take the plunge and make a purchase, a first-time investor understandably can get at least a little nervous about the details. The purpose of this chapter is to take some of the mystery out of buying stocks, bonds, or mutual funds. Along the way, I alert you to some pitfalls that you want to avoid.

Buying Stocks

The most common way to buy stock is to deal with a broker, which can be either land-based (the kind with folks who work in offices downtown) or in cyberspace (accessed via the Internet).

Choosing a broker

The first big choice you need to make is deciding which kind of broker you are going to deal with: full-service or discount.

If you believe that you are going to need a lot of advice, a full-service broker will probably better serve you. If you are making your own decisions about stocks, by all means use a discount broker. Discount brokers charge much lower commissions than do full-service brokers.

Many discount brokers have both electronic and "bricks and mortar" systems of operation. If you discount broker is on the Web, you can enter your order electronically and receive confirmation the same way. Some discount brokers have branch offices where you can sit down with a broker and discuss your investment objectives and goals.

Either way, you can obtain commission costs and product information by visiting a discount broker's Web site, by calling their phone number (usually toll-free), or by stopping by the branch office.

In addition to discount commissions, most discount brokers also offer other products and services, such as mutual funds, IRAs, research reports, bonds, and others.

Full-service brokers are paid by the commissions they earn on buying and selling stocks and other products for clients. This arrangement can lead to a tendency on their part to recommend frequent trading of stocks rather than pursuing a "buy and hold" strategy. This advice can put their interests in conflict with yours. So if you use a full-service broker, avoid miscommunication by making sure that she or he knows that you are not interested in frequent trading but in buying good stocks and holding them for the long term.

You may be better off if you find a good financial advisor to guide you on stock purchases and perhaps on other aspects of your financial program. These advisors often work for a flat fee on an hourly basis.

If you decide to work with a full-service broker, you have to choose a broker one way or another. How do you make this choice? You probably select a broker pretty much the same way you select a doctor, a lawyer, or other professional.

You ask people for recommendations. You look in the phone book. You see ads in the paper or on TV. After you acquire a list of potential brokers, take the process at least one step further. After you get several names, make some calls.

Call their offices and ask about account minimums and commission costs. Find out how convenient their services may be. If you're put on hold for longer than a few minutes or the broker asks to call you back but never does, he or she may not be the broker for you.

Narrow your choices down to two or three brokers and then interview each of them. Make several copies of the worksheet in Table 7-1, and keep them handy when you conduct your final interviews.

Sooner or later, you will get on a mailing list that is sold to brokers. Then you start getting unsolicited calls. All brokers have a good line and can be very persuasive. My recommendation: Find a financial planner in your area and deal with her or him face to face. A good financial planner whom you trust can be a very helpful to you as you work to achieve your financial goals.

Table 7-1: Questions to Ask a Prospective Broker

Question	Answer
How long have you been a broker?	
What type of training/ education have you received?	
How much money does it take to open an account (account minimums)?	
What are your commission costs to buy and/or sell stocks?	
What investment strategy do you recommend for a first-time investor?	
Which stocks have you and/or your firm recently recommended?	
How have these stocks performed?	
Can you provide me with two or three professional references?	
a.	
b.	
c.	

Signing a customer service agreement and setting up an account

After you figure out which broker you want to use to place your order, get back in touch with that person.

The broker will ask you to fill out an application, called the *customer agreement*. You can't avoid filling out this application. No broker can deal with you until you have provided him or her with information about yourself and your financial situation and goals. From the start, the broker will need accurate information to process stock purchases and, regrettably but necessarily, to keep the IRS informed about all the money you make from your investments.

The application requires you to provide some common personal information such as your name, address, tax identification number (social security number for most people), current job (if employed), your bank, and an estimate of your net worth.

If you are working with a full-service broker, you need to answer some broad questions about your investment goals and the kinds of stocks you are considering for investment.

Some very personal questions about your finances and goals may puzzle you or even turn you off, but brokers require this information for good reasons. A full-service broker is required by regulation to provide stock advice appropriate to the client's situation. This is often referred to as the "know your customer" rule.

There are two other aspects of the customer agreement that you should be aware of. The first is extensive and detailed information about how you will pay for your purchases and what happens if you are late in paying or don't pay at all. This part of the application is complex and legalistic.

I don't want to exaggerate the complexity of the agreement in general. It is long and detailed, but your broker should be willing to answer your questions. The securities industry is closely regulated, and you can be quite sure that the customer agreement is not intended to deceive you. It just takes patience to wade through it.

If you can't figure out what some parts of it mean, be persistent in asking your broker to explain the difficult parts to you. This could be a good test of whether you have picked the right broker. You will have lots of questions all along the way. Don't deal with a broker who doesn't have the time or inclination to work with you.

Warning

Make sure that you read and understand the customer agreement before you sign it. Don't be rushed into signing it.

Almost all of the customer service agreements currently in use require that you, the client, sign away your right to sue the broker if you believe you actually have been wronged. You will almost certainly be informed that if you have a dispute or problem, you must take it to arbitration for resolution.

Some brokers, especially Internet-based brokers, may require that when you establish your account with them, you also set up an account with sufficient funds in it to cover anticipated purchases. The brokerage then pays you interest on the funds you deposit with them.

Placing an order

Placing an order for stocks is simple. You need to know just two things: the name of the stock and the number of shares you want to buy.

If you are dealing with a live broker, the usual process is to place your order by phone. If you are dealing with an

Internet broker, the transaction is made on your computer screen and you provide the same information that you would phone in to a broker.

Under federal regulations, the buyer must pay for stock purchases within three business days. Brokers are very concerned to see that you pay within this period because they can be penalized or disciplined if payment deadlines are not observed.

After transacting your order, your broker tells you what the total charge is and sends you a written confirmation. (You can also check the Web site for your filled order, or call your broker on the phone.) The charge includes the price of the shares, the broker's commission, and usually some small fees. You then have three business days to get your payment to the broker. Both discount and full-service brokerages require that money be in the account within three business days.

Many investors find it more convenient to have funds in a money market fund at the brokerage before a trade is placed in order to meet the three-day requirement.

Use an overnight delivery service to deliver your payment. Sometimes full-service brokers provide clients with prepaid overnight mailers to use in sending payments. These services almost always deliver checks in a timely way, and they also have the means to precisely track when and where your payment was delivered.

Finding out about fees

The fees related to the purchase of stocks are few and easy to understand. You'll be required to pay some kind of commission both when you buy and when you sell stocks, probably an annual account maintenance fee (usually not very large), and small paperwork fees.

Table 7-2: Fees Differ from Broker to Broker

Transaction	Brokerage	Number of Shares	Transaction Fee	Per-Share Fee	Total Fee
Purchase XYZ company stock	Broker #1	100	$19.95	$0.25	$34.95
Purchase XYZ company stock	Broker #2	100	$19.95	None	$19.95

The biggest fee is the commission on purchases. Because of the competition from online discount brokers, commissions have been falling. Flat-rate charges of under $20 are starting to appear. Rates this low were unknown 10 years ago. The practice of paying commissions as high as 4 or 5% of the amount of the purchase are disappearing. Table 7-2 shows the importance of shopping around.

Some full-service brokers negotiate commissions. Be sure to ask and be sure to take the commissions and other fees into consideration when you select your broker.

Purchasing Bonds

Buying bonds is a lot like buying stocks. You just get in touch with your broker, set up your account, and place your order. If you already have an account with a broker, whether land-based or Internet, you shouldn't have to fill out any additional paperwork to buy a bond. The one account should allow you to purchase stocks, bonds, and mutual funds as well. Unless you are going to concentrate most of your investment money in bonds, there's usually no need to select a broker who specializes in this kind of security.

You do, of course, have to pay for any bonds that you purchase. You pay in the same way and timeframe as with stocks (within three days of placing the buying order). Fortunately, you don't get charged much in the way of miscellaneous fees when you buy bonds. These fees vary with the brokerage, but in almost all cases they are very small (sometimes less than $1 per transaction).

Commissions on bonds are about in the same range as those for stocks — high with full-service brokers and lower with discount and Internet brokers. Because investors show much less interest in bonds, competition has not yet brought bond commissions down to the very low levels that are paid for stock transactions on the Internet.

The Internet doesn't have many Web sites devoted to information about investing in bonds. There is, however, one outstanding site that more than makes up for the lack of numbers: the Bond Market Association site at www.investinginbonds.com. This Web site offers advice on buying bonds, explains how bonds fit into a balanced portfolio, and answers just about any question you might have about bonds.

Bonds trade on a type of OTC market, and most trade without securities symbols you see on securities that are traded on an organized stock exchange, like the New York Stock Exchange. Therefore, the investor has to tell the broker the type (tax or tax-free), how long (time) the investor will hold the bond, and state the investor's risk parameters. Most brokerages (discount and full-service) maintain a bond-trading department in order to meet varied customer needs and preferences.

Purchasing Mutual Funds

When you are ready to invest in a mutual fund, you can either work through a broker or, in many cases, you can buy directly from the mutual fund company. Many funds offer a toll-free number for placing orders, and you can buy shares of their funds.

Unlike stocks, you don't have to specify the number of shares you want to buy. You tell the fund company or broker that you want to invest a stated amount, and the fund or broker tells you how many shares you will get. Unlike stocks, mutual funds sell partial or fractional shares.

A mutual fund company can't sell you shares of a fund unless you have first received the prospectus for that fund. Whether you call or request the prospectus on the Web, you have to give your name and address. Fund managers need this data to prove that they have fulfilled their obligation to supply you with a prospectus.

When you begin to look into mutual funds, pay close attention to those that come in families — preferably big families. The term *family* refers to companies that offer several different kinds of funds. How big is big? Think in terms of ten or more funds. You can spot these families easily by looking at the mutual fund reports in the business section of your daily paper. You typically see some kind of headline in the columns followed by a list of funds offered by a particular firm. It's easy to spot the big families at a glance; these include Fidelity, Oppenheimer, T. Rowe Price, and Vanguard.

Families of funds that charge commissions (also called *loads* or *load charges)* provide the opportunity to switch among their funds without paying additional commissions. You can save considerable money with this option over the long term. Make sure to check out this possibility.

A mutual fund has professional management, which comes at a price. You, the investor, pay for this management, either through commissions you pay when you buy or when you sell and other fees that you are billed for periodically. These fees reduce your return on investment and can run as high as 7 to 8% a year, but 2% or lower is more common.

No-load funds don't charge sales loads. No-load funds are available in every major fund category. For details, see Chapter 3.

Although not all mutual fund companies charge commission, you need to know that the term "load" is often used in two ways. One is to specify commission charged when you buy a fund (referred to as *front-end load)*, and the other refers to commission charged when you sell your shares in a fund (known as *back-end load)*.

Many investors wonder why they should pay a commission to buy shares of a mutual fund when they can buy a similar fund without a commission. The answer is that, in most cases, there's no good reason to buy a load fund rather than a no-load fund. Several studies have indicated that the performance of the two types of funds doesn't differ. Unless you come across that rare case in which the performance of a load fund is so superior that it compensates for the load, save your money and buy no-load funds.

Almost all mutual funds charge some kind of annual fee. Analysts tally all these up into one measure called the *expense ratio*, expressed as a percentage of the invested funds. Expense ratios range from about 0.75% to 2%, but a few charge as much as 7%. The fund's prospectus discloses the current schedule of fees.

Beware of any load fund with a high expense ratio. Avoid funds that charge a back-end load. These high fees and loads are a large drain on an investment's overall return; few funds deliver performance consistently high enough to offset high expenses.

CHAPTER 8
MONITORING YOUR PROGRESS

IN THIS CHAPTER

- How to monitor your investments
- Which indexes you need to track
- What to expect from the markets' highs and lows

This chapter tells you how to assess the performance of your investments — or those you plan to buy — relative to their peers. It also provides you with tools to determine how the stock and bond markets, and the mutual funds that invest in them, are doing overall.

Checking Up on Savings Accounts, Money Market Accounts, and CDs

In Chapter 2, I qualify these investments as entry-level, or low-complexity investments. The same holds true for monitoring their progress.

Savings accounts

Monitoring your savings account is a lot like monitoring your checking account. You receive statements from the institution (bank, credit union, or savings and loan) that tell you your balance including accrued interest. Many institutions also have a telephone number — often toll-free — that allows you to access balance information by using your account number and your personal code number. In addition, more and more institutions have online banking that allows you to access your account information from your computer.

Money market accounts

Like savings accounts, you can access your money market account balance information either by reading the statements you regularly receive, by telephone, or via Internet connection to your account.

Certificates of deposit

When you invest in a certificate of deposit, you receive an actual document that indicates the principal you invested, the interest rate, the length of time of the investment, and the final amount you will receive. Some institutions include your balance information on the statements you receive from other accounts you have with them, but not all do that.

Possibly the most important thing to keep in mind with your CD investment is to keep track of the dates, because right around the time your CD matures you will receive a notice giving you the option to roll over the money from that account into an identical CD. You must respond during the 10-day period just prior to your maturation date or else it automatically rolls over.

If you miss that 10-day window of opportunity to cash in your CD, your investment automatically rolls over into an identical CD account and the financial penalty for withdrawing that money before it matures can in some cases cost you the amount you gained through interest.

Looking at Performance: The Indexes

An *index* is a statistical yardstick used to gauge the performance of a particular market or group of investments. By tracking average prices or the movement of prices of a group of similar investments, such as small or large company stocks or corporate bonds, an index produces a benchmark measure against which you can assess an individual investment's performance.

Think of using an index the same way that you may use a list of comparable home sales when you shop for a house in a neighborhood. If the list of comparable homes shows you that the average three-bedroom colonial sells for $189,000, you can't expect to buy a similar house for too much less than that. At the same time, you don't want to pay too much more. In the same respect, the benchmarks produced by an index show you a reasonable performance target.

Remember

A *return* is an investment's performance over time. If you're looking at performance for a period of time, say five years, look for an average annual return. If the same mutual fund returned 10% over the course of those five years, its average annual return would be 10%. Its *cumulative return*, which simply totals an investment's performance year after year, would be 50% for those five years.

If an investment's performance over the course of a year is vastly superior or inferior to the appropriate index's return, you'll want to know why. Your investment may be outpacing its peers because it's a lot riskier. A mutual fund, for example, may invest in stocks or bonds that are far riskier than other funds it may resemble. On the other hand, an investment may be lagging its peers simply because it's a poor performer. Bear in mind, however, that you have to build a performance history over time to determine the character of a particular investment. Notice that in Figure 8-1, the mutual fund is performing below average, which may prompt you to sell that investment.

The following sections offer a look at the indexes that are likely to come in handiest as you try to determine expected performance from your investments.

Start by tracking an index that represents or follows your stock or mutual fund. After you become familiar with that index, then pick up another index to follow. Be careful not to follow too many indexes, though — it can become confusing and time-consuming.

Figure 8-1:   A poor performer.

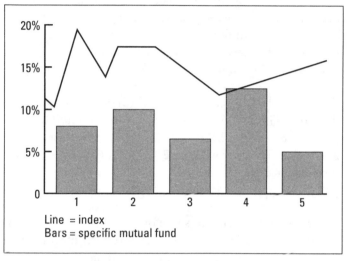

Line = index
Bars = specific mutual fund

The Standard & Poors 500

Also called the S&P 500, the Standard & Poors index, which most professional money managers say that they use as the benchmark against which they measure their own investing prowess, is the one that has become the dominant benchmark in U.S. investing in recent years.

Although the S&P is not really the appropriate measure of performance for bonds or the stocks of small-sized companies, nor the apt standard against which to judge international investments, the index is still used to gauge these investments' performances anyway.

The S&P 500 tracks the performance of 500 stocks, comprised of 400 industrial companies, 40 utilities, 20 transportation companies, and 40 financial firms. A committee at S&P reviews the companies periodically and may replace up to 30 for reasons that include, for example, bankruptcy.

The performance of the 500 stocks is run through a computer software program that calculates a daily measure of the market's rise or fall as well as an overall performance figure. These are the numbers you hear reported on the nightly news, see in the newspapers, and can view on your computer screen if you log on to a personal finance Web site.

The S&P tells you the average performance of the stocks in the index. This performance is reported as both numbers and percentages. If the S&P goes up, your newspaper might report that "the S&P went up 2 points or 6% today." When the stock market is doing well the numbers and percentages go up. When it's doing poorly, they go down.

The S&P 500 is home to some of the hottest stocks of the late 1990s, including AOL and Dell, the latter of which gave investors an unrivaled 79.7% average annual return, not for a day, not for a month, but for 10 years. With so much fanfare, the S&P has become the index to beat for mutual fund managers. Outperforming it is cause for celebration — only 1 out of 10 mutual fund managers do so in any five-year period.

The Dow Jones Industrial Average

The Dow Jones Industrial Average tracks the performance of 30 companies that are among the largest companies and some of the most venerable stocks the U.S. stock market has to offer. If you own one of these stocks, such as Exxon or IBM, you'll want to know how your stock is faring compared to the average.

The results of the Dow are reported daily in newspapers across the country and on new sites and financial Web sites. The results, which tell readers the average performance of the stocks in the index, are reported as both numbers and percentages. If the Dow goes up, your newspaper might report that "the Dow was up 4 points or 10% today." When the index goes up, investors are actively buying stocks and the stocks covered by the index are going up in value.

The Dow Jones is known all over the world. Still, it only tracks 30 stocks, and none of them can be considered high tech, so for 1999 and beyond, critics agree that the Dow is hardly the measure of the U.S. stock market's total success, the way it once was. It has slipped a bit behind the times. It does, however, serve as a daily report on how well the U.S. economy is doing. And it's important to look at it relative to its index peers, the S&P and Nasdaq, to get a sense about whether certain slices of the stock market are faring better or worse than others.

The Dow Jones Industrial Average is price-weighted — giving companies with a higher stock price more weight regardless of their size. Because of price-weighting, one company's stock can pull the index up or down significantly, even if that direction doesn't reflect the performance of the majority of the index's stocks. That price-weighting doesn't mean you can ignore the Dow Jones Industrial Average, which follows the performance of giants such as AT&T, and General Electric, but you should understand how the average is determined.

The Nasdaq Composite Index

In some senses, the Nasdaq Composite Index is sometimes seen as a competitor to the S&P, but the Nasdaq Composite is actually very different. For starters, Nasdaq measures the stock performance of 5,500 companies, nearly half of them in the telecommunications and high-tech arena, and all of them found in the Nasdaq market. The index includes companies such as Apple, Intel, MCI Communications, Cisco, Oracle, Sun Microsystems, and Netscape.

As a result, the Nasdaq index is a good deal more volatile than, for example, the Dow Jones Industrial Average and, perhaps, the stock market at large. It's also home to some of the bigger success stories of the 1990s — many of which are technology firms. The higher the potential for return an investment has, the more the risk it carries.

Just like the Dow Industrial Average and the S&P 500, the Nasdaq Composite gives the average performance of the stocks in the index both as numbers and percentages. If Nasdaq goes up, your newspaper might report that "Nasdaq was up 1 point or 3% today."

Although it will be increasingly important for investors to watch the Nasdaq Composite in the days ahead and the performance of some of its key stocks, it's equally important to look at Nasdaq in relation to the S&P 500 — and even the Dow — to get an overall sense of how the stock market is doing. For example, if you are a short-term trader (day trader) then the Nasdaq is where you want to be. The Nasdaq stocks can offer great potential for profit and, unfortunately, for loss, as well.

The Wilshire 5000

Want a good look at how the overall U.S. stock market is doing? The Wilshire 5000 tracks a huge universe of stocks — in fact, it lists almost every publicly listed stock, including those listed on the New York Stock Exchange, the American Stock Exchange, and the Nasdaq Composite. That's a pretty definitive look at the large-, medium-, and small-company stock markets.

This is not a must-read index, especially on a daily basis, but it is an index investors want to at least know about and have the option of viewing once in a while. It's the largest index going. It gives an investor a broad sense of how the U.S. stock market overall is faring and in which direction stocks are headed. More mutual funds have also started investing in stocks listed in the Wilshire 5000, which gives investors total U.S. stock exposure.

S&P Mid Cap 400

The S&P Mid Cap 400 index measures the performance of 400 medium-sized companies. If you're interested in investing in mid-size companies, or mutual funds that do — and there are a number of success stories in the mid-sized range — this is a good benchmark to use to gauge your own success.

The Russell 2000

The Russell 2000 is the most widely used benchmark for the smaller company market. (Other small company performance indexes include the S&P Small Cap 600, the Wilshire Small Company Growth Index, and the Wilshire Small Company Value Index.)

The Morgan Stanley Capital International Emerging Markets Index

The Morgan Stanley Capital International Emerging Markets Index looks at smaller companies that are operating in up-and-coming and also sometimes highly volatile developing markets around the world.

The Morgan Stanley Capital International Europe, Australia, Asia, and Far East (EAFE) Index

The Morgan Stanley Capital International Europe, Australia, Asia, and Far East (EAFE) Index, considered one of the more prominent, tracks more than 1,000 foreign stocks in 20 countries. This is the big daddy for international investors and money managers. It tells you how the international stock market is faring, and if you own stock or a mutual fund that invests globally, how you're doing in comparison.

Lehman Brothers Aggregate Bond Index

As the name suggests, the Lehman Brothers Aggregate Bond Index represents an aggregate of the performance of a number of bonds, including U.S. Treasury bonds and corporate bonds. For investors in U.S. bonds or bond funds, this is the benchmark for relative performance and the direction of the market.

Lehman Brothers Long-Term High-Quality Government/Corporate Bond Index

As its name suggests, the Lehman Brothers Long-Term High-Quality Government/Corporate Bond Index looks at the universe of higher-rated government and corporate bonds. To make it onto the index, a bond must have a maturity or duration of 15 years or more and a rating of A or better from Moody's.

If you're interested in making long-term investments in high-quality bonds, this benchmark gives you an idea of the type of performance you can expect and the way the market is faring right now.

Remembering that performance is relative

Everything is relative, regardless of which investment performances you're measuring. What may have been great performance a year ago may be considered good, bad, or indifferent today, depending on how the particular market you're invested in is doing.

Warning

Unless you have evidence of other negative indicators, don't knee-jerk into selling an investment just because its performance lags behind an index one year. You're investing for the long-term. What's underperforming its index this year may well bounce back next year.

The trick to using indexes is to be able to definitively tell how well the performance of your investments stack up against their peers in the market you're in. With that know-how, you can answer questions like: Is this stock's performance average? Is this mutual fund's performance above average? Is this bond's performance poor?

How does your performance compare with the indexes? Although you don't want to be 50% or more off the indexes or benchmarks for your investments, lagging 10% to 20% behind is nothing to sneeze at. For example, if in 1998 your investments came in 20% under the S&P 500's 28% performance, you would have reported more than a 22% return. Could you live with that? You should be happy to. With a 20% return, you'll more than double your initial investment in four years. These are the kinds of years you come to live for as an investor. And you'll be glad you built a portfolio rather than investing in just one or two stocks that may have entirely missed this increase in value.

Looking Rationally at Market Highs and Lows

You're investing hard-earned money, so you want to enjoy a sense of comfort and confidence in your investments' potential to perform as expected *over time*. I emphasize the phrase *over time* because chasing short-term performance can drive you crazy.

Investments can look mighty risky if you track their performance every day. In contrast, risk tends to flatten out a bit if you look at it year to year. In fact, since the late 1920s, few classes of investments have lost money over a 10-year period. Of course, some individual investments have lost money, but the general rule applies: Holding on to investments for a longer period of time will reduce your exposure to losses.

Do you want to avoid undue risk? Invest for the long-term — or, at the very least, five years. If you need to tap your investments earlier than that, stick to shorter-term cash equivalents, such as money market mutual funds (which invest in high-grade bonds with shorter maturities), certificates of deposit, and money market accounts.

Learning how to gauge the market is different from thinking you can predict the market. No one — not even the most savvy broker — knows with any real certainty how well or how poorly the market will fair in the future.

Reaching Your Goals

After you start investing, monitor your progress to ensure that you're on track. Make the anniversary of your first investment your day of financial reckoning (or at least that month).

When the day arrives, sit down and take an earnest look at what you're investing in, how much you're investing, whether or not your goals have shifted or changed completely, and whether or not you're saving enough (and earning enough on your investments) to reach your goals.

The ultimate measure of your portfolio isn't whether or not you're beating the benchmarks. It's whether or not you're reaching your goals. Are you? For example, if you determined at the outset that you needed to invest $500 a month and earn an average annual return of 9%, are you hitting your goal?

If you're meeting or beating your goals, you're in great shape. If you're not, identify what's wrong. Maybe you're not investing enough. You may have to pay off some bills so that you can find more money in your household budget to invest. Or you may find that your 401(k) needs greater funding so you have to increase the percentage of your pay you contribute each week or month.

To ensure that your investment plan is a workhorse that's pulling its weight, feed it. As you get raises at work, or come into "found" money — maybe a small inheritance, a bonus at work, or a tax refund — consider investing some or even all of these funds in your portfolio.

Knowing When to Sell

Of course, maybe one or more of your investments isn't performing up to your standards. This kind of letdown happens to the best of us, and you can count on a disappointment once or twice in your investment life. When underperformance hits home with one of your investments, take a deep breath and try to figure out what's happening.

Figuring out how long to hold on to an investment that isn't producing any growth is a challenge. You have to first determine what is keeping the investment on the rocks. The following sections offer a look at why an investment may be underperforming.

When you sell a stock, bond, or mutual fund, make sure that you find a suitable replacement and don't leave the cash lying in your checking account, where it may be pilfered away by life's daily expenses.

Is the economy the reason for your investment's slump?

Is the entire market taking its lumps? If so, your then investment isn't immune. If one or more sectors of the stock market are taking a licking, consider the impact to your stock, bond, or mutual fund. A sluggish economy, or one that is in retreat, can play havoc with investments. Investments are long-term endeavors. Don't sell just because of an economic downturn. You'll take a loss.

An economic downturn can create a buying opportunity if it sends the price of stocks spiraling downward.

Is your stock falling behind?

If a stock is struggling, look at the company. Forget about what's happened to date for a moment. If you discovered the company again today, would you buy it? Do some future analysis on the company's prospects. Don't let your answer be clouded by negative feelings about the past few months or years. If you bought the stock because you believed that the company was well-positioned for a turnaround due to new and competitive products or services, sales, profits, or other facets of its financial position, hang on a bit more. The last thing you want to do is take a loss on a stock that may turn around a few days or months after you give it the boot.

At the same time, if you decide you wouldn't buy the stock again today, or some of the economic reasons that attracted you to the stock in the first place haven't panned out, selling is okay.

Is your bond slipping behind?

If a bond is doing poorly, maybe because the stock market is booming (typically, when the stock market is doing well, bonds are lagging, and vice versa), ask yourself what cost you can expect from hanging on to the bond until maturity. Compare that expense with what it will cost you to sell the bond. If interest rates rise substantially, say to 15%, and you're hanging on to a bond paying 4%, you might well be better off selling the older issue and buying a new bond.

Is your mutual fund fumbling?

If your mutual fund isn't performing up to snuff, then look at the fund manager's style. If the stock market is growth-oriented and your manager is a value manager who looks for bargains, you may be wise to hang on. Value-style investing comes in and out of favor, and you wouldn't want to miss the upside. Of course, if an inept mutual fund manager is the only reason you can find for the lagging performance, you can sell. Just try to wait until a fund's performance has been impaired for at least two years in order to avoid unnecessary losses.

CHAPTER 9

NOW WHAT?

IN THIS CHAPTER

- Determining your comfort level
- Diversifying your investment approach
- Finding out what you need to know about taxes

Right about now, you're probably feeling some sense of satisfaction. You've begun the enviable journey of building an investment plan and realizing your financial goals. Beyond the load of information you've absorbed already, some additional common-sense concepts can make your investing experience more productive and less mysterious. A few tricks of the trade also can help you become a more effective investor by guiding you around some of the pitfalls that trip up even the most earnest and dedicated investors.

Starting and Staying with a Diversified Investment Approach

The goal of diversification is to minimize risk. Instead of putting your eggs in one basket by investing every dime you have in one stock, one bond, or one mutual fund, you should diversify.

Diversification is a strategy for investing in a wide array of investments that ideally move slightly out of step with each other. For example, an investment in an international mutual fund might be doing poorly while an investment in a U.S. stock mutual fund is doing well. By investing in different sectors of the investment markets, you create a balanced portfolio. Parts of that portfolio should zig when other sections zag.

Table 9-1 shows the power of diversification by examining how three different diversified portfolios of money markets, bonds, and stocks can fare over time. The table also give you a concrete idea of the investments that should go in a portfolio based on your own tolerance for risk. They're also a good way for you to measure whether your own portfolio is diverse enough for your own tolerance for risk or loss.

Table 9-1:   Three Models of Diversification

	Lower Risk/ Return Portfolio	Moderate Risk/ Return Portfolio	Higher Risk/ Return Portfolio
Makeup	20% money markets, 40% bonds, 40% stocks	20% money markets, 30% bonds, 50% stocks	20% money markets, 0% bonds, 80% stocks
Return for best year	22.8%	28.1%	35%
Return for worst year	−6.7%	−13.4%	−19.6%
Average annual return	9%	10.1%	10.9%

It's important to determine the percentage of stocks, bonds, and cash you want in your portfolio. In the stock and bond categories (or mutual funds that invest in these assets), it's also important not to load up on any one sector of the economy. So steer clear of the temptation to invest in three technology mutual funds, four Internet stocks, or six junk bonds — even if they're paying more than other investments.

The saying "no pain, no gain" also applies to the investment experience. You can avoid the prospect of experiencing any pain at all by investing only in money markets and CDs that are federally insured. The price to be paid for that strategy:

You may never lose money in the traditional sense, but you never gain much either, which means that you can still fall behind. You also run the risk of falling behind because of inflation, which eat ups approximately 3% of your purchasing power each year. If you only earn 4% or 5% a year on your savings or investments, you'll have a hard time preserving the capital you have, let alone growing it.

Developing a Dollar Cost Averaging Plan

No one can afford to have his or her investing plan be forgotten or relegated to the back burner. You need to set up a plan for making set, regular investments. This way, you can ensure that your money is working for you even if your best intentions are diverted.

Dollar cost averaging is a way to ensure that you make fixed investments every month or quarter, regardless of other distractions in your life. Dollar-cost averaging is a simple concept: You invest a specified dollar amount each month without concern about the price per share or cost of the bond. The market is *fluid* — the price of your investment moves up and down — so you end up buying shares when they're inexpensive, some when they're expensive, and some when they're somewhere in between. Because of the commission cost to buy small amounts of stocks or bonds, dollar cost averaging is better suited for buying mutual funds.

If you have a 401(k) plan at work, you already have experience with dollar cost averaging. You fill out the forms for the plan and direct your payroll department to take a certain dollar amount or percentage of your pay every payday and use it to buy the mutual funds, stocks, bonds, and/or money market account you've selected. Investing this way is important for your retirement accounts and your financial plans: It's the only way most of us can grow our money in a consistent manner.

In addition to helping you overcome procrastination about saving for investments, dollar cost averaging can help you sidestep some of the anxiety many first-time investors feel about starting to invest in a market that can seem too over-heated or risky. With set purchases each month or quarter, you buy shares of your chosen investments regardless of how the market is doing.

Dollar-cost averaging isn't statistically the most lucrative way to invest. Because markets rise more often than they decline, you're better off saving up your money and buying stocks, bonds, or mutual funds when they hit rock bottom. But dollar cost averaging is the most disciplined and reliable way to invest. Consider this: If you set up a dollar-cost averaging plan now, then in 10, 20, or 30 years, you'll have invested every month in between and accumulated a pretty penny in the interim.

Most mutual funds let you start out on a dollar cost averaging plan (or automatic investing plan, as they're also called) for as little as $50 or $100 a month. The only catch is that you have to sign up to allow the fund to take the money from your checking account each month. To find out if the funds you're interested in offer the service, look for the information in their prospectuses or call their toll-free shareholder services phone number.

Investing with Your Eye on Taxes

Unfortunately with investing, as with just about any other activity that generates income, gains are taxable. That downside doesn't mean that you shouldn't try to invest successfully. But you should realize that you do pay taxes on investment gains. Consider the following:

Savings accounts

The gains on simple savings accounts, CDs, and money market accounts are taxed as income at the local, state, and federal level. Banks and financial institutions report these gains to the IRS and state tax offices, just as all investment gains are reported.

Mutual funds

With mutual funds, unfortunately, you have to pay tax each year on the capital gains and dividends that the fund distributes to each of its shareholders. You also have to pay taxes on your own gains when you sell shares — another reason for a long-term buy-and-hold strategy. The exceptions are funds that invest in U.S. securities. You still have to pay federal income tax on any gains, but you're free of state and local tax in most situations.

Although some people believe that municipal bond funds are free of federal income tax, that's only true of municipal bond investments themselves. You pay taxes on capital gains on any profits that a municipal fund makes from selling bonds.

Stocks

With stocks, you don't pay taxes on your gains until you sell your shares — a feature which fans of stock investing say is a clear advantage in the long run. The downside, however, is that when you do cash in shares down the road, your tax bracket or the tax rate may have increased.

If you do have a stock loss (which means a stock is worth less than what you bought it for), but the stock is one you want to own, consider selling the stock and rebuying shares at a lower price. The IRS allows you to consider this a *wash sale,* so you won't have to pay capital gains tax. Note that you must wait 31 or more days before you can buy back the stock or else the IRS doesn't allow the deduction.

Bonds

Price appreciation (if any) on a bond — whether it is a corporate, government, or municipal bond — is taxable when the bond matures. Interest on municipal bonds is exempt from federal tax, but may be subject to state and local tax (depending on if you live in the state or locality doing the issuing). Interest on U.S. government bonds is exempt from tax at the state level, but taxable at the federal level.

If you buy a bond from Fannie Mae or Ginnie Mae (the quasi-government agencies that guarantee mortgages), then gains are taxable at the local, state, and federal level.

Tax-deferred investing

Don't forget to take advantage of any form of tax-deferred investing available to you. Max out on the retirement plans offered to you at work (such as your 401(k) plan). Investing in this way really does boil down to a choice of paying yourself or paying the IRS.

With retirement plans such as a 401(k), you enjoy the added bonus of being able to deduct your contributions, up to a maximum of 15% of what you earn, from your income each year for tax purposes. Now that's hard to beat. The maximum amount that you can deduct depends on the plan. Some plans allow 8%, some 10%. But no plan is allowed, by law, more than 15%.

Contributions made to a 401(k) plan are deductible from gross income for income tax purposes. If you do your taxes yourself, you deduct your overall annual contribution from your gross income. If an accountant or attorney does your taxes, she or he does the deduction for you.

Just as hard to beat is the Roth IRA. If you have adjusted gross income under $95,000 as an individual, you can tuck away $2,000 in a Roth IRA each year and begin to take distributions tax-free when you hit the age of 59½. If you're married and you and your spouse have a combined adjusted gross income of $150,000 or less, you can tuck away $4,000 a year. Unlike regular IRAs, Roth IRAs allow investments even if you're enrolled in an employer-sponsored retirement plan. The same goes for self-employed folks. With the Roth, you get tax-free capital gains every year, and you get to take withdrawals tax-free when you hit retirement age at 59½, provided you've had the account for at least five years. Figure 9-1 shows the qualifying incomes for investing in a Roth IRA.

Figure 9-1: Roth IRA qualifying incomes.

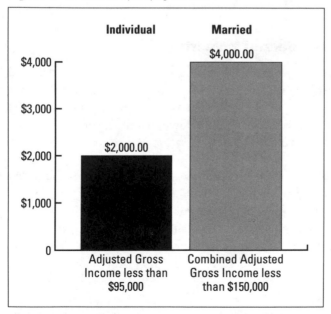

Deductions for an IRA differ in that you take a dollar amount deduction, not a percentage of your gross income. The maximum deduction for an IRA is $2,000 per individual, If you qualify for the plan.

The price you pay for tapping your retirement accounts early

Don't do it. I repeat, please do not take money out of your retirement accounts on a whim, say, when you're changing jobs or feel the need for an extravagant vacation. If you make the withdrawal anyway and you're not age 59½ yet, you can look forward to the double whammy of both taxes and a penalty. First, you have to pay tax on any capital gains in the account. Then, you have to pay the IRS a 10% penalty. The same holds true for early withdrawals from regular IRAs.

Remember

The IRS has agreed to waive the early withdrawal penalty on qualified withdrawals made from Roth IRAs before age 59½ — these include first-time home purchases and college education for the kids — but you still have to pay the taxes.

Borrowing from retirement plans can be as bad or worse because you pay interest to borrow your own money. And you lose the interest you would have earned on these accounts.

Pecking away at retirement savings is no way to build your nest egg. If you're changing jobs and don't want to leave your money in the former employer's 401(k) plan, roll the money directly over to an IRA at the fund company or broker-dealer where you have your other investments. Fill out a form that your former employer provides directing them (or their plan provider) to roll your plan money into an IRA at your next firm. Make sure that you set up the account with the new firm first.

CLIFFSNOTES REVIEW

Use this CliffsNotes Review to practice what you've learned in this book and to build your confidence for making your first investment. After you work through the review questions, some possible scenarios, and the fun and useful projects, you're well on your way to achieving your goal of becoming a successful first-time investor.

Q&A

1. What is the difference between a money market fund and a money market account? _____
_____

2. If you feel comfortable with more risky investments, what mutual fund type may be right for you?
   a. Balanced funds
   b. Equity income funds
   c. Aggressive growth funds

3. An established, old company usually pays dividends
   a. Regularly
   b. Not at all
   c. Infrequently

4. What does the term "bear market" mean?_____
_____

5. If you want your investment to reduce your tax payments, you may choose to invest in
   a. Corporate bonds
   b. Municipal bonds
   c. Treasury bonds

6. At what age can you access your IRA funds without paying any penalty?

   a. 60

   b. 59½

   c. 70

7. What four things should first-time investors not do?

_____

_____

_____

_____

8. What are three of the indexes used to measure stock and bond performance?

_____

_____

_____

9. One way the Roth IRA differs from a regular IRA is that you

   a. Can make early withdrawals without penalty.

   b. Can't touch money in the fund until you are 75.

   c. Are taxed and pay a penalty for early withdrawals.

Answers: (1) A money market fund is a mutual fund that invests in low-risk, stable investments. It is not FDIC insured and is one of the more popular types of mutual funds even though its yields can be lower than those of other types. A money market account is a bank account insured by the FDIC for up to $100,000 that tends to earn more interest than a standard savings account. (2) c. (3) a. (4) A bear market is a market in which stock prices drop 20% or more from their previous highs. (5) b. (6) b. (7) Invest for the short-term; speculate or choose risky investments; choose only one type of investment; neglect to do research. (8) S&P 500, Dow Industrial Average, Nasdaq Composite Index (9) a.

Scenarios

1. You want to invest for retirement, and you and your spouse or partner have a combined income of $100,000. You decide to invest in an IRA. Because you don't want to pay capital gains tax if you withdraw money early, you pick the _____.

2. You just graduated from college, and your aunt has given you $200 in U.S. savings bonds. You need money for the security deposit on your first apartment, but also want to start a nest egg. Your best move is to _____ _____.

3. The used car you bought five years ago is starting to show signs of age. You've been saving money in a savings account for major future purchases. Your local mechanic has told you that the car will last just another two or three years. The money in your savings account isn't enough for a down payment on another car, but could be if it earned more interest. Two of the best accounts to move your money into are _____ _____.

Answers: (1) Roth IRA. (2) Hold the bonds until maturity because they will be worth more then than the face value now. (3) A CD or money market account because they tend to earn more interest than a standard savings account.

Consider This

■ Did you know that some stocks have a dividend reinvestment plan (DRIP)? Some stocks can be set up to automatically reinvest any dividends toward additional shares of that stock. This plan can save on brokerage and other fees.

■ Did you know that starting to invest even a small amount when you are in your 20s can make a significant difference for your retirement funds? Due to compound interest, people who start investing even a $100 a month at age 25 stand to gain considerably when they retire at 60 or 65. People who start to invest the same amount at 35 or 40 can't earn as much due to fewer years of interest.

Practice Projects

1. Investigate different interest rates at banks and credit unions. Get information from several different banks and credit unions for six-month, one-year, and two-year CDs. Compare the rates and then decide which is the best option for you.

2. Look through financial magazines, such as *Fortune, Business Week, Forbes,* or *Money.* Find a few companies that sound like potential investments; research them by using Morningstar and Value Line. Do the company reports present a different profile from what the articles led you to believe? Which research tool was most useful? Would you invest in any of these companies?

3. Look at your long-term retirement goals. What are you doing now to achieve them? Research the different types of IRAs and analyze which is best for you. Check to see if you are eligible for a 401(k) plan and find out about the plan's options. Which is better for you — an IRA, a 401(k), or perhaps both?

CLIFFSNOTES RESOURCE CENTER

The learning doesn't need to stop here. CliffsNotes Resource Center shows you the best of the best — links to the best investing information in print and online. And don't think that this is all we've prepared for you; we've put all kinds of pertinent information at www.cliffsnotes.com. Look for all the great resources at your favorite bookstore or local library and on the Internet. When you're online, make your first stop www.cliffsnotes.com, where you'll find more incredibly useful information about investing. Happy hunting!

Books

This CliffsNotes book is one of the many great books on investing published by IDG Books Worldwide, Inc. So if you want some great next-step books, check out these other publications:

CliffsNotes *Investing in Mutual Funds,* by Juliette Fairley, gives you a more in-depth look at investing in the world of mutual funds. IDG Books Worldwide, Inc., $8.99.

CliffsNotes *Investing in the Stock Market,* by C. Edward Gilpatric, helps you further improve your investing prowess with specific information about investing in stocks. IDG Books Worldwide, Inc., $8.99.

Investing Online For Dummies, 2nd Edition, by Kathleen Sindell, helps you unlock all the investing resources and capabilities available in the vast world of Cyberspace. IDG Books Worldwide, Inc., $24.99.

Investing For Dummies, 2nd Edition, by Eric Tyson, provides tips and hints about investing that can turn you from a first-timer into a power investor. IDG Books Worldwide, Inc., $19.99.

Mutual Funds For Dummies, 2nd Edition, by Eric Tyson, enlightens you with over two decades of the author's mutual fund knowledge. Check out the sample portfolios for ideas on your own mutual fund investments. IDG Books Worldwide, Inc., $19.99.

Finding books published by IDG Books Worldwide, Inc. is easy. You can find them in your favorite bookstores (on the Internet and at a store near you). We also have three Web sites that you can use to read about all the books we publish:

- www.cliffsnotes.com
- www.dummies.com
- www.idgbooks.com

Internet

Check out these Web sites for more information about mutual funds, stocks, bonds, real estate, savings accounts, IRAs, and more:

Investing In Bonds.com, www.investinginbonds.com provides numerous links to a host of other bond Internet sites. Stop here on your way to all the best bond information online.

Apartments.com, www.apartments.com offers listings for apartments, condos, and townhouses across the United States. Many listings include video tours.

Lipper Inc., www.lipperweb.com sets you up with performance data and analysis of the mutual fund industry. You can get the industry news you need to stay on top of all your mutual funds.

Department of Labor Pension and Welfare Benefits Administration, www.dol.gov/dol/pwba/ focuses on planning and investing for retirement. You can search for an investment advisor, find an investment firm, or find available advisors who are registered in your state.

Money.com, www.money.com has some of the best fund and stock analysis in the industry.

Financenter.com, www.financenter.com/calcs.html is worth a visit to discover some of the best savings and loan calculators going.

The Street.com, www.thestreet.com comes through with real-time quotes, financial reporting, and analysis.

The next time you're on the Internet, don't forget to drop by www.cliffsnotes.com. We have created an online Resource Center that you can use today, tomorrow, and beyond.

Send Us Your Favorite Tips

In your quest for learning, have you ever had a sublime moment when you figure out a trick that saves time or trouble? Perhaps you realized that you were taking ten steps to do something that could have taken two. Maybe you found a little-known workaround that gets great results. If you've discovered a useful tip that helps you invest more effectively and you'd like to share it, the CliffsNotes staff would love to hear from you. Go to our Web site at www.cliffsnotes.com and click the Talk to Us button. If we select your tip, we may publish it as part of *CliffsNotes Daily*, our exciting, free e-mail newsletter. To find out more or to subscribe to a newsletter, go to www.cliffsnotes.com on the Web.

INDEX

NUMBERS & SYMBOLS

401(k)s
advantages of, 26
basics of, 24
employer contributions, 25
investment choices, 25, 26, 27
options when leaving employer, 27
role in retirement planning, 27, 28
tax deferral, 25, 107

A

annual adjusted gross income, 30

B

bear market, 40
Bond Market Association, 85
bonds
basics of, 52, 53
bond mutual funds, 36
buying, 83, 85
current yield, 57
face value, 57
first steps, 67, 68, 69
identifying potential investments, 56, 57, 58
indexes
Lehman Brothers Aggregate Bond Index, 96
Lehman Brothers Long-Term High-Quality Government/Corporate Bond Index, 96
interest rate, 57
issuers, 53
knowing when to sell, 99, 100, 101
maturation date, 52, 57
monitoring progress, 96
price, 57
principal, 52
research sources
Bond Market Association, 85
Investing In Bonds.com, 115
Moody's, 68
Standard & Poors, 68
risk

corporate bonds, 56
municipal bonds, 55
U.S. Government Securities, 55
selling at discount, 57
selling at premium, 57
taxes, 58, 107
types of
corporate bonds, 55
municipal bonds, 55
savings bonds, 55
Treasury bills, 54
Treasury bonds, 54
Treasury notes, 54
zero-coupon bonds, 54
yield to maturity, 58

C

CDs. See certificates of deposit
certificates of deposit
defined, 20
drawbacks, 23
FDIC insurance, 21
interest rates, 22
matching to goals, 21
maturation date, 20
minimum deposit requirements, 20
monitoring progress, 89
returns compared to saving accounts, 21
risk, 22
rolling over, 20
shopping around, 75
taxes, 23
time periods, 20
withdrawal restrictions, 20, 23
checking accounts
linking to money market accounts, 19
compound interest
calculating, 9
defined, 8
Rule of 72, 9
corporate bonds, 55

D

Department of Labor Pension and Welfare Benefits Administration Web site, 116
diversification, 34, 70, 102, 103
Dogs of the Dow, 66
dollar-cost averaging, 104, 105
Dow Jones Industrial Average, 92, 93

COMING SOON FROM CLIFFSNOTES

Online Shopping

HTML

Choosing a PC

Beginning Programming

Careers

Windows 98 Home Networking

eBay Online Auctions

PC Upgrade and Repair

Business

Microsoft Word 2000

Microsoft PowerPoint 2000

Finance

Microsoft Outlook 2000

Digital Photography

Palm Computing

Investing

Windows 2000

Online Research

Have you ever experienced the thrill of finding an incredible bargain at a specialty store or been amazed at what people are willing to pay for things that you might toss in the garbage? If so, then you'll want to learn about eBay — the hottest auction site on the Internet. And CliffsNotes *Buying and Selling on eBay* is the shortest distance to eBay proficiency. You'll learn how to:

■ Find what you're looking for, from antique toys to classic cars

■ Watch the auctions strategically and place bids at the right time

■ Sell items online at the eBay site

■ Make the items you sell attractive to prospective bidders

■ Protect yourself from fraud

Here's an example of how the step-by-step CliffsNotes learning process simplifies placing a bid at eBay:

1. Scroll to the Web page form that is located at the bottom of the page on which the auction item itself is presented.

2. Enter your registered eBay username and password and enter the amount you want to bid. A Web page appears that lets you review your bid before you actually submit it to eBay. After you're satisfied with your bid, click the Place Bid button.

3. Click the Back button on your browser until you return to the auction listing page. Then choose⇨Reload (Netscape Navigator) or View⇨Refresh (Microsoft Internet Explorer) to reload the Web page information. Your new high bid appears on the Web page, and your name appears as the high bidder.